BRIEN FOERSTER

A BRIEF
HISTORY OF THE INCAS

FROM RISE,
THROUGH REIGN, TO RUIN

LIMA - PERU

DEDICATION

I dedicate this book to those teachers who shaped and informed my life and love of Indigenous people and philosophy.

My Uncle Jim Gilbert, who taught me carving in the native styles of the people of the west coast of Canada, Dick and Tippy Fuchs, Linda Siegel, David Hart, Reg Ashwell, and Geoff Swift, who were my greatest and dearest sculpture patrons.

My mother, Ann, who has always supported my every endeavor, and applauded every dream that I have chased, no matter how crazy. And my true love, Irene Mendoza, whose love and wisdom are as large as the monuments of her Incan forebears.

Finally, I wish to honour all of the Indigenous people of the world, red, black, yellow and white, and the children of these great people who remember where they come from, and carry in their hearts and minds, the noble truths of their ancestors.

May we all walk together, guided by the warmth and light of Inti, our Father, gently and with good intent and purpose on our Mother, Pachamama.

Brien Foerster
Lima Peru

A BRIEF HISTORY OF THE INCAS

FROM RISE, THROUGH REIGN, TO RUIN

The main purpose of this book is to give an overview, concise yet thorough, of the origin of the Inca Civilization, its achievements and splendour, and the reasons why it was overtaken and destroyed by a relatively small group of Spanish soldiers of fortune.

The majority of early written accounts of the history and culture of the Inca have been penned by people of European (mainly Spanish) origin, and Peruvian Native and/or Mestizo (mixed blood) who were heavily influenced, one might even say corrupted and censored, by the Spanish establishment; both church and state.

As the old saying goes, 'history is written by the winners'.

As the Inca had no written form of history, most of the information in this book has been gleaned from the so-called winners' perspective. However, some of the oral traditions have been written down, and have been included as much as possible.

Since I have accessed many different sources, I feel that by piecing together this historical puzzle, with hopefully an unbiased approach (you may differ) a somewhat balanced account may be possible to display.

As I am neither of Peruvian nor Spanish descent, I have no reason to slant this story one way or the other; I want to know and offer you the truth, as close as I can come to it.

ORIGINS

The most common stories relating to the source of the Incas, where they came from, are that they originally lived around or near Lake Titicaca, geographically located approximately 150 miles southeast of Cuzco.

Oral traditions are often very poetic in nature, and many of the traditional Incan accounts say that Manco Capac, and his blood sister Mama Ocllo Huaco, who were Children of the Sun God Inti, "rose" from the waters of Lake Titicaca, and were instructed by their celestial father to bring order back to what had become a chaotic world.

These two were not only brother and sister, but also husband and wife. Manco was instructed to teach the people the arts of agriculture, and Mama Ocllo the arts of weaving and spinning.

To say that they "rose" from Lake Titicaca is probably a poetic way of saying that they came from that area, their culture rising akin to a renaissance.

In terms of archaeological evidence of an advanced civilization existing at or near Lake Titicaca before the time of the Inca, one only has to visit the massive sacred ceremonial center of Tiahuanaco (or Tiwanaku), located approximately 13 miles from the eastern shore of Titicaca.

A modern view of Tiwanaku at sunrise

In terms of stone architectural technology, it easily rivals, if not surpasses, that of the Incas.

The age of this site is widely and hotly debated; most commonly, however, it is believed that the Tiahunacan culture rose around 600 BC, and fell into decline sometime soon after 1000 AD. A much more explosive yet compelling theory is that of Arthur Posnansky, a German-Bolivian scholar, who dated the site at 15,000 BC. His theory, based on 50 years of study, uses the science of archaeo-astronomy to compare the alignment of the solstices present day, as compared to the past.

View of the main temple complex of Tiwanaku, with a Viracocha sculpture in the central background

Sculpture of Viracocha at Tiwanaku, near the famous Gateway Of The Sun

By most accounts, the first Inca arrived in Cuzco about 1100 AD, so, in terms of chronological time, Tiahuanaco makes sense as the site of origin of the Inca. It has also been written by many authors that the leaders at Tiahuanaco were priest kings, who were driven out of their homeland by the Huari, a more war-like and barbaric people, about 1000 AD. It is also known that the soil of Tiahuanaco was or had become, by this time, very infertile, and thus was incapable of growing crops of any great quality or quantity. This was, in part, due to an extreme El Nino, that caused the area around Tiwanaku to experience a 40 year drought.

Manco and Ocllo carried with them a golden wedge or staff called Sunturpaucar, a cage with a sun-bird who could give good advice, and other sacred objects. They were instructed by their father Inti to test the land's fertility as they traveled, for cultivation. Where the golden staff entered the soil easily was the place told that they should found their new home.

A VERY stylized painting of Manco Capac and Mama Ocllo rising from the waters of Titicaca

Near the site of the present day Coricancha in Cuzco, Manco Capac plunged Sunturpaucar into the soil, where it not only entered the ground easily, but completely disappeared below the surface. Thus, the founding of a new city, and center of a new culture, had begun. From a purely practical standpoint, the Sacred Valley would have been chosen due to its relatively close proximity to their ancestral lands, and the fact that it has flat, highly arable soil, nurtured by a major river, the Urubamba, fed by glacial waters from the Andes.

This valley is a major "bread basket" to this very day.

Of course, Manco Capac and Mama Ocllo did not travel alone. Oral traditions speak of there having been 4 pairs of brothers and sisters, all related, who started the journey from Titicaca together, but the other three pairs, for various reasons, did not complete the journey. They were collectively called the Ayar brothers and sisters. The four sets of brother-sister/wife-husband probably relate to four clans of people.

Whether the other three sets of brother-sisters were killed, or became subordinate to Manco and Ocllo is uncertain. What is known is that Manco became the first supreme or Sapa Inca; the father of the Inca civilization.

The Sacred Valley outside of Cuzco, photographed from the highway winding down to the valley floor

Salkantay, one of the Apus, or guardian spirit mountains near the Sacred Valley

The names and timelines of the Sapa Inca are as follows

Hurin Dynasty:

Manco Capac	1200-1230
Sinchi Roca	1230-1260
LloqueYupanqui	1260-1290
Mayta Capac	1290-1320
Capac Yupanqui	1320-1350

Hanan Dynasty:

Inca Roca	1350-1380
Yahuar Huacac	1380-1410
Viracocha	1410-1438
Pachacutec	1438-1471
Tupac Inca Yupanqui	1471-1493

Huayna Capac	1493-1527
Ninan Cuyochi	1527
Huascar	1527-1532
Atahualpa	1532-1533

In each case, the eldest son inherited the throne of the father. This continued, in unbroken succession, from Manco Capac to Huayna Capac. After this began a brutal and pivotal civil war, which will be dealt with in detail later on in the book.

This painting, like all those made in post-Inca times, is speculative as regards to the facial features of the Sapa Inca.

Three major tribes lived in the Cuzco valley area when Manco Capac and Mama Ocllo arrived. They were the Sawasiray, the Allkawisas and the Maras, who had an alliance that the Inca joined.

The political power of this confederated state was divided between two groups: the Hanan, which controlled most of the political and religious power, and the Hurin, which was in charge of the military. At this time, the Inca were put in charge of the Hurin aspect of the confederation, but maintained their adherance to their God Inti.

During the 14th century, the leaders Sinchi Roca, Lloki Yupanqui, Mayta Capa, and Capac Yupanqui led several wars against neighbouring tribes of Cuzco. By the time that Capac Yupanqui died, his son Inca Roca had gained enough power to become Hanan, and thus controlled all aspects of political, religious, and military affairs.

After Inca Roca's death, the Inca state began to decline under the rule of Yahuar Huacac. However, the next Sapa Inca, Viracocha, stabilized the state, which now reached a 50 km radius from Cuzco. At this time the Chanka tribe had expanded its territories south of Cuzco, and along with an alliance of other southern tribes, made a move to attack Cuzco.

The Chanka army greatly outnumbered that of the Inca, and as the battle started, the Chanka placed a statue of their founder in front of their troops. During the battle, the Inca took control of the statue, and perhaps seeing this as a terrible omen, the Chanka deserted the battlefield.

The next Sapa Inca, Pachacutec, whose name roughly translates as "earth shaker" began the great expansion period of the confederation. During his reign, he and his son, Tupac Inca Yupanqui brought much of the Andes mountains, roughly modern day Peru and Ecuador, under Inca control.

Stylized painting of the Sapa Inca Pachacutec

UNA BREVE HISTORIA DE LOS INCAS

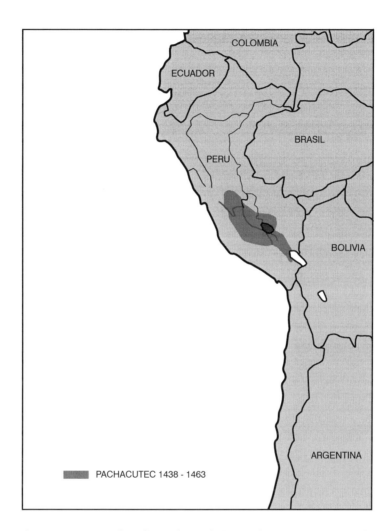

PACHACUTEC 1438 - 1463

Pachacutec was the founder of the Tahuantinsuyu; a federalist system which consisted of a central government with the Sapa Inca at its head, in Cuzco, and four provincial governments with strong leaders: Chinchaysuyu (NW), Antisuyu (NE), Contisuyu (SW), and Collasuyu (SE) Pachacutec is also regarded as the builder of Machu Picchu.

What sets the Inca's method of territorial expansion at this time, and perhaps earlier, from other cultures is both intriguing and very clever. They formed a confederation, not an empire, and this point can not be emphasized enough.

Empires tend to grow based on the subjugation and destruction of other groups and nations; not only their political systems and military, but also their belief systems. A confederation is an alliance of groups and or nations.

Pachacutec sent spies to regions that he wanted to expand into. These spies brought back reports on the political organization, military might, and wealth of the prospective confederation candidates. He would then send messages to the leaders of these lands extolling the benefits of joining the confederation, offering them presents of luxury goods such as high quality textiles. Benefits to the candidate lands included access to the extensive Inca road system, some 15000 to 25000 miles in size, and the goods and services that were within the realm of the Inca's sphere of influence.

The benefits to the Inca were access to goods and services that were particular to that region, and tolls paid for use of the roads.

Most accepted the rule of the Inca, and acquiesced peacefully. It was only when a perspective candidate refused to join the confederation that military force was used.

It was traditional for the Inca's first born son to lead the army, and from the time of Manco Capac to Huayna Capac the first born son inherited the title of Sapa Inca.

Pachacutec's son Tupac Inca began conquests to the north in 1463, and continued them as Inca after Pachacutec's death in 1471. His most important "conquest" was the kingdom of Chimor (Chan chan is a remnant of that culture) the Inca's only serious rival on the north coast of Peru. Tupac Inca then expanded into modern day Ecuador and Colombia.

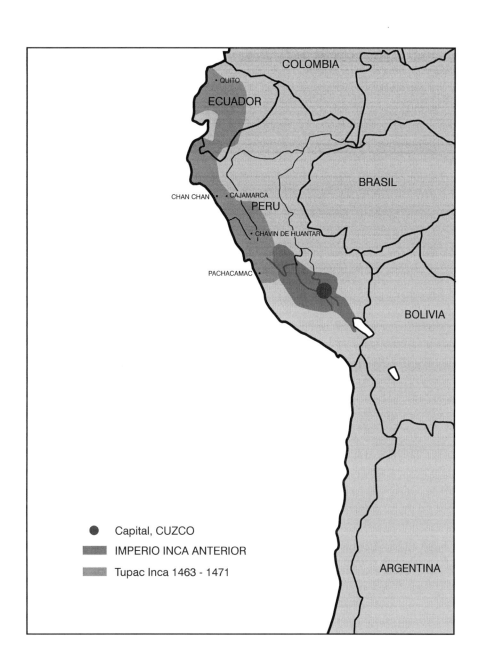

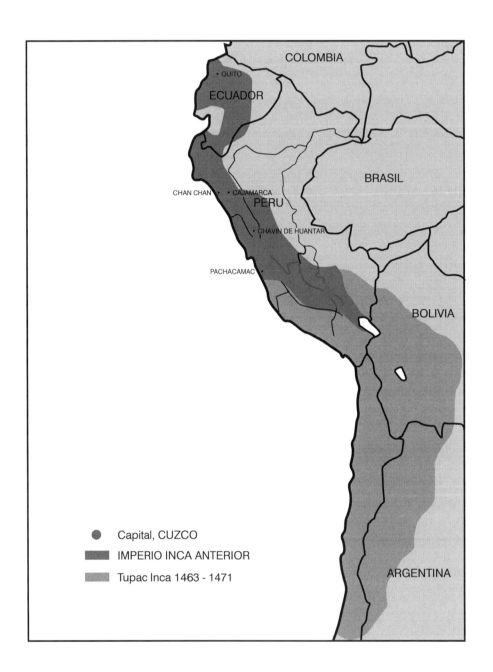

COLOMBIA

• QUITO

ECUADOR

BRASIL

CHAN CHAN • • CAJAMARCA

PERU

• CHAVIN DE HUANTAR

PACHACAMAC •

BOLIVIA

● Capital, CUZCO

IMPERIO INCA ANTERIOR

Tupac Inca 1463 - 1471

ARGENTINA

Tupac's son, Huayna Capac, added significant territory to the south. At its height, Tahuantinsuyu included Peru and Bolivia, most of what is now Ecuador, a large portion of what is today northern Chile (as far south as Santiago) and extended into corners of Argentina and Colombia.

At this time, Tahuantinsuyu was the largest confederation or empire in pre-Columbian America.

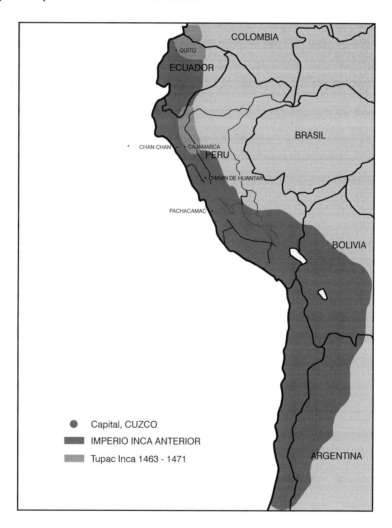

Huayna Capac spent his later years in Quito, Ecuador, where his Ecuadorian wife (his principal wife, or Qoya, lived in Cuzco and was the mother of Ninan Cuyochi and Huascar) bore him a son, Atahuallpa. Huayna Capac died in 1527, supposedly from small pox which had made its way through the native communities from Panama, and Ninan Cuyochi then became the Sapa Inca, as he was the first-born son.

Ninan Cuyochi was, however, Sapa Inca for only a year, as he too succumbed to small pox. It is possible that Huayna Capac knew that Ninan Cuyochi's reign would be short, and he supposedly declared that Huascar and Atahuallpa should share power, a definite break in the previous arrangement of passing the title of Sapa Inca from father to first born son.

In 1527, after the death of Ninan Cuyochi, Atalhuallpa became sovereign of the ancient kingdom of Quito, and Huascar was given the rest of the Tahuantinsuyu. Civil war broke out between the two brothers at some point between 1527 and 1532. Huascar was eventually captured by Atahuallpa in 1532 and executed.

Atahuallpa became Sapa Inca for only a period of months, when he was executed by the Spanish in 1533, having arrived on the Peruvian shores a year previously.

The death of Ninan Cuyochi ended the traditional rite of Sapa Inca succession, as I stated above. With the death of Huascar and Atahuallpa, the Tahuantinsuyu fell into a state of disarray, and the confederation began to crumble. In order to restore some sort of order, the Spanish installed Manco Inca Yupanqui, the younger brother of Huascar (from a different and lesser Cuzqueña mother) as Sapa Inca; in essence a puppet Sapa Inca. A feud developed amongst the Spanish; Pizarro, the Spanish leader, was fighting resistance and tribal separation to the north of Cuzco, while his associate Diego de Almagro decided to claim Cuzco as his own property. Yupanqui decided to use this intra-spanish feud to his advantage, recapturing Cuzco in 1536, but the Spanish soon retook the city.

Manco Inca Yupanqui then retreated to the mountain retreat of Vitcos or Vilcabamba, close to Machu Picchu, where he and his followers remained for another 36 years, sometimes raiding the Spanish or inciting revolts against them. In 1572 this last Inca stronghold was discovered, and Tupac Amaru, Manco's son, was captured and executed, bringing the great Inca confederation and civilization to an end.

Without the Sapa Inca being present as the political, religious, and military figurehead and center of power, it made it relatively easy for the Spanish to seize control of the masses of Peruvian people; and for political and military alliances to fracture and crumble.

In 1589, Don Mancio Serra de Leguisamo, the last survivor of the original conquerors of Peru wrote of the Inca:

'We found these kingdoms in such good order (upon our arrival) and the said Incas governed them in such wise manner that throughout them there was not a thief, nor a vicious man, nor an adultress, nor was a bad woman admitted among them, nor were there immoral people. The men had honest and useful occupations. The lands, forests, mines, pastures, houses and all kinds of products were regulated and distributed in such sort that each one knew his property without any other person seizing it or occupying it, nor were there law suits respecting it…the motive which obliges me to make this statement is the discharge of my conscience, as I find myself guilty. For we have destroyed by our evil example, the people who had such a government as was enjoyed by these natives. They were so free from the committal of crimes or excesses, as well men and women, that the Indian who had 100,000 pesos worth of gold or silver in his house, left it open, merely placing a small stick against the door, as a sign that its master was out. With that, according to their custom, no one could enter or take anything that was there. When they saw that we put locks and keys on our doors, they supposed that it was from fear of them, that they might not kill us, but not because they believed that anyone would steal the property of another. So when they found that we had thieves among us, and men who sought to make their daughters to commit sin, they despised us'.

I would like to move on now to a more thorough description of life in the Inca world prior to the arrival of the Spanish; when the confederation was at its prime, during the reign of Pachacutec, founder of the Tahuantinsuyu.

The name of Peru was not known to the native people; just as the name of the United States was not known to the native peoples of that geographic region. Peru was a name given by the Spanish and originated, it is believed, in a misapprehension of the native name for river, or "Pelu".

Tahuantinsuyu can be translated as the "four corners of the Incan World". At its peak, the Tahuantinsuyu totalled about 906, 500 square kilometers. It extended to Colombia to the north, Chile to the south, west to the ocean, and east into the Amazon Basin.

The center was Cuzco, geographically, as well as politically, spiritually, and militarily. It was indeed called by the Inca the navel or belly-button of the world. Four great roads ran out of the center of Cuzco, from the present day Plaza de Armas, to each of the four Suyus.

Cuzco itself was divided into four quarters, and the various tribal groups that gathered there from the distant parts of the confederation lived in the quarter nearest to the lands that they had come from. Cuzco was, in essence, a miniature image of the Tahuantinsuyu.

The head of government, the military, and all spiritual matters was the Sapa Inca. His advisors, the Amauta, were each an expert in a particular field of knowledge; agriculture, law, military matters, etc. From an early age, the Sapa Inca was educated by many Amautas, perhaps as many as 300, so that he would have a strong grasp of each of the subjects pertinent to the running of an efficient confederation.

The Sapa Inca, as well as his immediate blood family, were

recognized as the "Children Of The Sun"; figuratively, or perhaps even literally descending from the Sun God Inti. Thus, he in essence had a "divine right to rule". All other important governmental, religious, and military high offices were held exclusively by members of the Inca elite.

Painting by an early Spanish artist depicting a Sapa Inca, with his ceremonial axe in hand and holding his God Inti in the other

The whole of the Tahuantinsuyu was divided into three parts in regards to land usage; one for the Sun, another for the Inca, and the last for the people. The lands assigned to the Sun furnished a revenue to support the temples and maintain the costly ceremonies of Incan worship and the priesthood. Those reserved for the Inca went to support the royal state, and the various government departments. The remainder of the lands was divided, per capita, in equal shares among the people.

Daily life of the people of the Tahuantinsuyu revolved around three basic laws or principles: be truthful, be fair, and work hard. This was later corrupted by the Spanish as: don't lie, don't cheat, and don't be lazy; basically, they converted three positive principles to three that had negative connotations.

The productivity of the people, as a result of the obeying of the three principles, and the fact that practically every climatic condition existed within the Tahuantinsuyu, ocean, highlands and jungle being the simplest way to describe them, was a firm foundation on which the Tahuantinsuyu grew and thrived.

For example, there existed at that time, through brilliant cultivation and cross-breeding, over 2000 different types of potatoes alone, each one able to exist in a particular environment of altitude, soil condition, and rain fall.

Photo of a few of the myriad varieties of potatoes presently grown in Peru

Another genius stroke of the Inca was the development of a massive and extensive series of roads, estimated to be a system, at its peak, of between 15,000 and 25,000 miles in over-all length.

The two most considerable roads extended from Quito to Cuzco, and from Cuzco to Chile; in essence, one single road, estimated to being 1500 to 2000 miles in length, and 20 feet wide.

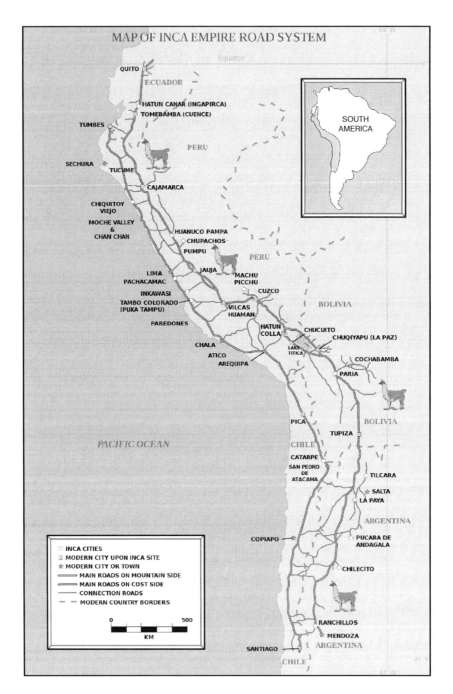

MAP OF INCA EMPIRE ROAD SYSTEM

SOUTH
AMERICA

Equator

QUITO
ECUADOR
HATUN CANAR (INGAPIRCA)
TOMEBAMBA (CUENCE)
TUMBES
PERU
SECHURA
TUCUME
CAJAMARCA
CHIQUITOY
VIEJO
MOCHE VALLEY
&
CHAN CHAN
HUANUCO PAMPA
CHUPACHOS
PUMPU
PERU
LIMA
JAUJA
PACHACAMAC
MACHU
PICCHU
INKAWASI
CUZCO
TAMBO COLORADO
(PUKA TAMPU)
VILCAS
BOLIVIA
HUAMAN
PAREDONES
HATUN
COLLA
CHUCUITO
CHUQIYAPU (LA PAZ)
CHALA
LAKE
COCHABAMBA
ATICO
TITICA
AREQUIPA
PARIA
PICA
BOLIVIA
TUPIZA
PACIFIC OCEAN
CHILE
CATARPE
SAN PEDRO
DE
TILCARA
ATACAMA
SALTA
LA PAYA
ARGENTINA
COPIAPO
PUCARA DE
ANDAGALA
CHILECITO

INCA CITIES
MODERN CITY UPON INCA SITE
MODERN CITY OR TOWN
MAIN ROADS ON MOUNTAIN SIDE
MAIN ROADS ON COST SIDE
CONNECTION ROADS
MODERN COUNTRY BORDERS

0   500
KM

RANCHILLOS
MENDOZA
SANTIAGO
ARGENTINA
CHILE

UNA BREVE HISTORIA DE LOS INCAS

Due to the rugged and varied terrain inherent in the landscape, ingenious suspension bridges were constructed from the tough fibers of the maguey plant, the resulting ropes being as thick as a human body, which stretched as long as 200 feet. Massive stone pillars were constructed on either side of the abyss or river to anchor the bridge, and wooden planking formed the bridge deck.

Pen and ink drawing of and Incan suspension bridge

Replica of an Incan rope bridge built in the Apurimac region, south of Cuzco

The other great road stretched from Cuzco, in the Andes, to the ocean, providing access to the abundant bounty of fish and other products from the ocean. At intervals of 12 miles Tambos, or inns were erected of stone. These provided accommodation for the travelers, be they Inca, military, merchants, or the Chasquis, who were the royal messengers.

The Chasquis carried not only the Quipus, ingenious knotted cords which were records both numerical and text, but also fresh food from the sierra, ocean, and jungle to the royal court. The Chasquis were stationed at intervals of approximately five miles, and acted in a relay fashion, thus efficiently carrying information and goods along the roads.

In order to have an efficient way of communicating verbally (as has been said the Inca did not have a written language) Quechua, or Runa Simi (the true native name) which was the language of the Inca, was made the official language of the Tahuantinsuyu. While each tribal group or district maintained its traditional language, the universal adoption of Runa Simi allowed the inhabitants of one part of the Tahuantinsuyu to communicate with others in another part, and, for the Inca and the governmental, religious, and military departments to communicate to all.

The construction of such a massive infrastructure clearly took place over centuries of time, if not millennia. The traveler to Peru, at least in my case, was told by various local people and tour guides that the Inca seemed to be responsible for building practically everything that was grand or complex in nature.

This is clearly false, and does not give credit to the cultures that preceded the Inca; clumped together under the name "pre-Inca". These cultures, some of which date back 3000 years in the case of the Chavin, or even 5000 years in the case of the inhabitants of Caral. These people, even at that distant time, had developed sophisticated trading routes, religious and philosophical expression, amongst other qualities.

The brilliance of the Inca was the inclusion of other cultures' qualities into their own; the melding of the best attributes of each group into a cohesive whole. Thus, the great Inca road system was clearly the result of linking, and then expanding earlier trade routes, for example.

What made this method of integration and evolution seamless during the time of the Inca was that each succeeding Incan monarch seemed desirous to tread in the path and carry out the plans of his predecessor. Great enterprises, such as a major road, that commenced under one Inca, was continued by another, and then possibly completed by a third.

A common language, efficient road system, and powerful, centrally controlled military ensured the stability of the Tahuantinsuyu. However, a universal religious belief system was also a vital tool to create a cohesive society.

As the Inca were the ruling class, and were descendants or "Children Of The Sun", Inti, the Sun God, was proclaimed as the highest expression of divinity for the Tahuantinsuyu. The sun, amongst other things, is a physical object that has universal appeal.

Stylized painting of Manco Capac and Mama Ocllo departing Titicac region

He is the energy source for all life on earth, and thus is a great symbol for being the source of energy and consistency, for he rises each morning, bringing light and heat to all of earthly existence.

The Inca did not force the belief in other deities or gods amongst the various tribal groups of the Tahuantinsuyu to be abandoned, however, Inti had to be adopted as supreme to all others. In fact, the sculptures and idols of lesser gods were not destroyed by the Inca, but were moved to Cuzco, and placed in special temples.

Inti was the symbol of the creative energy of the universe, but was not the creator himself. That was Viracocha, a being, whether physical or ethereal is not clearly known, that was the Creator God of the priest kings of Tiwanaku, and thus a deity worshipped for millennia before the Inca. As Inti was the energy of the Source, Viracocha was the intelligence of the Source.

Illustration of Viracocha (or Wiracocha) from relief carving at Tiwanaku

At some point in time, Viracocha was replaced, in name at least, by that of Pachacamac, a Creator deity that pre-dated the Inca, and most of the other native groups of Peru.

The other major celestial deity worshipped by the Inca was the moon, or Quilla, who was Inti's sister and wife. Therefore, as Inti represented the divine father, and was symbolized as gold, Quilla was the divine mother, and her symbol was silver.

Few temples or other religious structures were built by the Inca to venerate Viracocha or Pachacamac. Perhaps the grandest monument to Pachacamac existing today is the sprawling site that bears his name, located on the outskirts of Lima.

The most lavish and elaborate temples were dedicated and consecrated to Inti, and the greatest of these was the Coricancha, or "the place of gold " now called the Church Of St. Dominic, located in the center of present day Cuzco. Gold, in the figurative language of the people, was "the tears of the Sun", and every part of the interior of the temple glowed with massive burnished golden plates, studded with jewels. On the western wall there was a golden relief carving of massive proportions, studded with emeralds and other gems, with a human face and long ornate rays. It was so situated that the morning sun fell directly upon it as it rose, lighting the whole interior of the building.

The Corichancha in Cuzco. All that remains of the Inca temple is the fine stonework at the base

Also, the central courtyard was a true garden of gold; flowers, maize, and even llamas, life-size in proportion; all made of solid gold.

The head of all Incan religious shrines, temples, customs, and ceremonies was the High-Priest, or Villac Vmu. He was second only to the Sapa Inca in dignity, and was usually chosen, by the Sapa Inca personally, from his brothers. The title and role of Villac Vmu was for life, and all other high positions of a religious nature were solely chosen from the Sapa Inca's immediate blood family.

The equivalent of the catholic nun in the Incan religious system were the "Virgins Of The Sun", young maidens selected at a young age, and only of Incan blood. They lived in buildings, similar to convents, close to the Temple Of The Sun in each of the main cities, which in the case of Cuzco was the Coricancha.

Here they were instructed and cared for by elderly matrons, Mamaconas, in the arts of spinning and embroidery, woven wall hangings, and the apparel for the Sapa Inca and his household. All of these were made from the fine hair of the Vicuna.

Though called the "Virgins Of The Sun", they were brides of the Sapa Inca. At the appropriate age, the most gifted and beautiful amongst them shared his bed, and thereafter lived in the royal household. These royal "virgin brides" numbered often in the thousands.

'Science was not intended for the people, but for those of generous blood. Persons of low degree are only puffed up by it, and rendered vain and arrogant. Neither should such meddle with the affairs of government; for this would bring high offices into disrepute, and cause detriment to the state'. Such was a favourite saying of Tupac Inca Yupanqui, son of Pachacutec, and father of Huayna Capac.

High learning, like high office, was the exclusive domain of the Sapa Inca and his immediate blood relatives. The royal pupils were placed under the tutelage of the Amautas, or wise ones, and were instructed in all of the different kinds of knowledge that these teachers possessed. They studied the laws, and the administration of government, in which many were later on to take part. Also, they were given religious and probably military instruction, as well as detailed history of their ancestors and their achievements.

They were trained to speak Runa Simi, their mother language, with purity and elegance, and taught the science of the Quipus; the knotted cord system that has been mentioned earlier.

The Quipu was a cord about two feet long, composed of different coloured threads that were tightly twisted together, from which a quantity of smaller threads were suspended, like a fringe. The threads were of different colours, and were tied into knots. In fact, the word Quipu is Runa Simi for knot. The colours seemed to represent practical things; white being silver and yellow gold, but also abstract ideas as well; white signifying peace and red, war. But the main function of the Quipus was for arithmetical purposes.

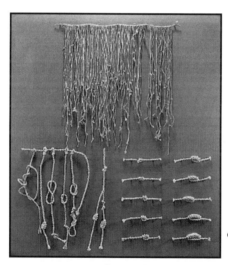

Examples of Quipus displaying knots representing numbers and other data

The knots represented numbers, and could be combined in such a manner to represent any amount required. The abacus used by the Chinese may be thought of as a similar instrument.

Officers were established in each of the districts, called Quipuca-mayus, or "keepers of the Quipus" and their job was to furnish the government with information on various important matters. One of the Quipucamayus was in charge of the revenues, for example, the amount of raw materials such as wool distributed amongst the labourers, the quality and quantity of fabrics made from it, and the amounts stored in the royal warehouses. This would also have applied to agricultural products, military hardware, household utensils, etc.

Another Quipucamayu would be in charge of births and deaths, marriages, the number of the populace qualified to bear arms, and other such details of life in all areas of the Tahuantinsuyu. Once a year the Quipus were forwarded to Cuzco, where experts trained in them would decipher the contents of each one. Thus, the government in Cuzco was provided with a mass of statistical information, carried along the efficient Inca road system by the swift-footed Chasquis.

Agriculture and soil maintenance were also carried out on a massive scale, and the population of the Tahuantinsuyu were well cared for in this regard.

The coast provided a bounty of seafood, and although the land along most of the sea-coast suffered from lack of rain, as it does to this day, a massive system of canals and subterranean aqueducts were built and maintained to carry water from lakes and rivers in the highlands to the coastal plains. For example, one aqueduct in the department of Contisuyu (south-west of Cuzco) was 400 to 500 miles long. In fact, there are aquaducts that date from the Nazca culture, approximately 1000 AD, that still function, carrying cool clear water from remote sources in the mountains to the dry desert lowlands.

As with many of the achievements of the Inca, they did not construct all of the aqueducts and canals in the Tahuantinsuyu, but also integrated and expanded on many existing ones.

As with the Nazcans, who were a thriving culture long before the Inca, the Chimu, builders of the massive adobe city of Chan chan on the north coast of Peru, had a very large and intricate canal system that supplied their population of at least 100,000 people.

In the more mountainous regions, where soil and water were plentiful, but the terrain was steep, terraces were constructed, again, on a massive scale. At the base of the mountain, the terraces could be several hundred acres in size, and would gradually decrease in depth towards the top of the mountain, where they would only be wide enough to accommodate a few rows of Native corn, or maize.

One of the finest examples of Incan terracing surviving to this day. This is at Machu Picchu

A fine example of this can be seen in the Sacred Valley outside of Cuzco, and especially in and around Pisac. In fact, one section of a mountain right behind the town of Pisac is not only completely terraced, but also forms the shape of a huge Condor.

Layout of terraces at Pisac. The Condor figure represented must be seen to be appreciated

The Tahuantinsuyu, having a great variety of climatic conditions, produced an amazing bounty of food. In the Amazon jungle (La Selva in Spanish) bananas and other tropical fruits were grown and harvested in great abundance. And high up in the Cordilleras, beyond the limits of the growth of maize, and other grains such as Quinoa, was to be found the potato; all 2000 varieties of them.

On the coastal arid plains, cotton was grown, thanks to the aforementioned aqueduct systems, and furnished the people with a clothing suitable to the milder latitudes of the Tahuantinsuyu.

In the higher elevations, such as Cuzco, wool was the material most suited to the manufacture of clothing. Of the four varieties of so-called Peruvian sheep, the llama, was and is the least valuable for its wool. Its primary function was that of a beast of burden, and although it can carry little more than 100 pounds, this is compensated

38

A classic symbol of Peru and the Andes, the llama

by its low maintenance requirements. It can live off of the moss and stunted plants in the highest parts of the Andes, and has the same water retention capabilities of the camel. Also, having spongy hooves with a single claw on each allows for sure-footedness.

During the reign of the Inca, caravans of up to 1000 llama were employed to carry food and other products from one part of the Tahuantinsuyu to another, along the great roads. This means 100,000 pounds could be in transit at any one time. The llama were and are very docile animals, as are its close cousin the alpaca, and thus were easily domesticated. The wool of the alpaca is finer and thus less "itchy" in nature than that of the llama, and was the one most used for the making of clothing by the populace.

The most highly prized wool was and is that of the guanaco and vicuna, who roamed freely in the highest elevations of the Andes. They were not easily domesticated, and were rounded up once a year,

The elusive and highly-valued Vicuna, whose wool was solely used by the Inca

presumably in the spring, and were shorn of their prized coat, without causing harm to the animal. The finest of the vicuna wool was reserved for the use of the Sapa Inca and his family.

Gold and silver jewellery, drinking vessels, and other utensils, as well as relief and three-dimensional sculpture, were both plentiful and of a high quality of craftsmanship. Iron was abundant in the ground, but was not used by the Inca. The tools used for working with gold and silver were stone or copper, and the most refined tools were made of bronze. Gold was plentiful in the streams and rivers, and gold ore was extracted in considerable quantities from the valley of Curimayo, northeast of Cajamarca. Silver was abundant in Porco, Bolivia, also known as Potosi. It is essentially a mountain of silver, which the Spanish later exploited to the detriment of the Native population, essentially working thousands of them to death.

The process of smelting both gold and silver ore was by means of furnaces built in elevated and exposed places, where the strong breezes from the mountains fanned the flames.

Amongst the greatest accomplishments of the Inca, architecture is clearly high on the list. Even to this day, after 500 years of European persecution and destruction, and the earthquakes that frequent the area, many of the greatest monuments ever constructed by the Inca still exist, and amaze the eyes.

Incan masonry excellence inside the Coricancha in Cuzco

The most obvious and intact example of Incan architecture, is, of course, Machu Picchu, reputedly built during the reign of Pachacutec (1438-1471). Its relative intactness is largely due to the fact that it was abandoned, most likely soon after the arrival of the Spanish, and lay hidden amongst the vegetation of its tropical location until its excavation, beginning in 1911, by Hiram Bingham.

Most of the monumental Incan architecture was made of granite, or porphyry; a hard igneous rock imbedded with crystals. The fact that near perfect joinery of such a hard substance could have been achieved with the shaping by such a soft tool material as bronze makes the construction of these great structures a mystery, and open to all sorts of theories, none of which make sense to me, personally.

Simplicity, symmetry, and solidity perhaps best describes the overall architectural style. Unlike the Maya or Aztec people to the north, in Central America and Mexico, the exterior of the Incan buildings were mainly left unadorned of carving, etc.

Yet, it is the amazing precision of their construction, and grand scale, that amazes visitors to this day. In present day Cuzco, for example, most of the major buildings made by the early Spanish, such as the prominent churches, were built on top of the foundations of the Incan royal palaces, temples, and governmental buildings.

Earthquakes over the centuries have toppled and sometimes completely destroyed the Spanish-built structures, but the Incan foundations remain untouched. One of the jokes in Cuzco is that the Spanish buildings were built by the "Inca-pables".

The author at the "cyclopean" stonework at Sachsayhuaman, outside of Cuzco

UNA BREVE HISTORIA DE LOS INCAS

As we all know, Christopher Columbus (Christobel Colon was his real name) was the first European generally recognized to have "discovered" the Americas, even though the Vikings had preceded him by 300 years, and the Phoenicians by possibly much more. He was of Italian origin, and was financed by King Ferdinand and Queen Isabella of Castille, Spain.

Between 1492 and 1521, the entire eastern coast of the Americas, from Labrador in present day Canada to Tierra del Fuego (the southern tip of South America) had been explored.

The main intent of European exploration at this time was to find a sea route to India and the Spice Islands. For centuries, Europe had been trading with India via land routes, and maritime access was desired in order to both expand trade, and make the movement of goods faster and more efficient.

About the year 1511, Vasco Nunez de Balboa, while in Panama, discovered that the local natives were in possession of small amounts of gold, which he very mush coveted.

A young native chief, observing Balboa's interest in the metal exclaimed "If this is what you prize so much that you are willing to leave your distant homes and even risk life itself for it, I can tell you of a land where they eat and drink out of golden vessels, and gold is as cheap as iron is with you".

Not long after this, he became the first European to discover and cross the isthmus that divides the Americas, namely, the location of the present day Panama canal. Upon seeing the Pacific Ocean, he claimed this hitherto unknown sea, with all that it contained, for the King of Castille, and that he would make good the claim, against all, Christian or infidel.

However, failing health prevented Balboa from being the one to discover Peru. It wasn't until 1524 that three men, colonists living in

Panama, were chosen by the Spanish Crown to undertake explorations in the Pacific, south of Panama. The one selected to lead this quest was Francisco Pizarro.

Monument to Pizarro in Trujillo, Spain

Pizarro was born in Trujillo, Spain, in approximately 1471. He was an illegitimate child, and received little care or attention from either

UNA BREVE HISTORIA DE LOS INCAS

of his parents. He was not taught to read nor write, and took on the occupation of being a swine herd.

However, his ambitions were much greater than this. With tales being circulated around him of the discovery and wealth of a New World in the west, beyond the seas, he made his way to Seville; the major port from which Spanish adventurers embarked to seek fame and fortune in these "New" lands.

He arrived in Hispanola in 1511, and by 1515 found himself on the Pacific coast of Panama, trading with the natives there for gold and pearls. His material wealth became meager at best, and in 1522, with the financial and logistical help of Diego de Almagro, a soldier of fortune, and Hernando de Luque, a Spanish priest, the aforementioned Pacific exploration mission was formed.

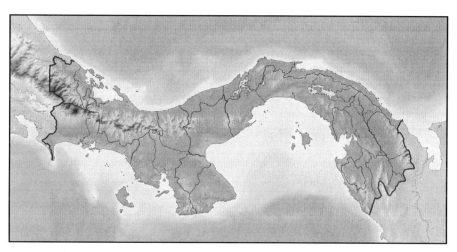

Map of Panama. The isthmus and location of the present day canal is in the center, top

Pizarro and Almagro, with their limited savings, bought guns and other weaponry, while Luque financed the purchase and outfitting of two small ships. 100 men, colonists from Spain who had arrived there with dreams of fame and fortune, but who had fallen very short of these goals, became the crew.

Assuming command, Pizarro embarked on the larger of the two vessels in November 1524. Almagro was to follow in the smaller ship at a later date.

Pizarro sailed south with difficulty, as it was the rainy season and the winds were against him, impeding his progress. His ship entered the river Biru (probably in present day Colombia) and the entire crew, except for the sailors, embarked to explore the territory. This area proved to be a massive tropical swamp, and was quickly abandoned.

Map of present-day Colombia

Travelling further south, Pizarro and his crew encountered more bad weather, and inhospitable terrain. Running low on food and drinking water, Pizarro decided to make camp on land, and send the ship back north to gather provisions on the Isla de Pearles (Isle Of Pearls) Panama.

It was thought that this re-provisioning voyage would take a few days, but actually took 6 weeks. Early on after the ship had left, Pizarro and his crew were suffering from starvation. Stumbling upon a small Indian village, the Spanish eagerly rushed in.

The frightened natives ran away into the dense brush, and Pizarro and his men devoured what food they could find; mainly maize and cocoanuts. The astonished natives, gathering confidence (as neither Pizarro nor his crew seemed to be hostile) inquired "why did they not stay at home and till their own lands, instead of roaming about to rob others who had never harmed them".

What Pizarro found especially interesting about these natives was that they wore gold ornaments; crude in workmanship but large in size. The natives explained that 10 days journey across the mountains to the south, there lived a great king whose lands, rich in gold, had been invaded by an even more powerful monarch; the Child Of The Sun. This invasion may have been the takeover of Quito by Sapa Inca Huayna Capac.

Their ship finally returned, fully provisioned, and so Pizarro set off again, south, hugging the coastline. The next Indian village they discovered seemed abandoned, and Pizarro and his men again availed themselves of the food and gold ornaments that they found in some of the dwellings. On travelling deeper inland, they came upon an even bigger Indian settlement, again seemingly abandoned. Once again gold ornaments were found, which they promptly confiscated.

However, unlike the earlier native encounters, the inhabitants of this settlement attacked Pizarro and his group, causing several casualties. Wounded and tired, Pizarro returned to Panama with the gold he had appropriated.

Pizarro obtained permission from the governor of Panama to embark on a second voyage, based upon the fact that he had found some gold, although not a lot. Once again his main financial backer was the priest Fernando de Luque.

In return for his advancement of funds for the journey, Luque was promised, under contract, to one third of all land, gold, silver, precious stones, and people that Pizarro and his partner, Almagro, conquered. Two vessels, larger than the previous two, were provisioned, and 160 men, once again the least fortunate of Panama's colonists, made up the crew, along with a few horses this time, and better armaments.

With finer weather, the two ships left port, and travelled farther south than on the first expedition. At a small village near Rio de San Juan, Pizarro surprised the villagers who fled, leaving a fairly large quantity of gold behind. Flushed with this success, Almagro was again sent back to Panama to find more recruits.

Meanwhile, Pizarro stayed on shore, and sent his ship's captain, Ruiz, to sail farther south. Shortly after setting off, Ruiz came alongside a large balsawood raft, equipped with a sail. The native inhabitants wore gold and silver ornaments, much more refined than those seen in earlier encounters, and woolen clothing of very fine texture, embroidered with birds and flowers, and dyed in brilliant colours.

Early Spanish drawing of Balsa craft with sails

Two of the natives stated that they were from Tumbes (northern Peru). Ruiz decided to detain some of the natives, including the two from Tumbes, and take them back to Pizarro. During the voyage, he and the crew taught the two Tumbes natives Castiliano, so that they might act as interpreters.

During the weeks that Ruiz was away, Pizarro and his small retinue of followers had decided to venture inland. He entered the lushness of the tropical jungle, where thick foliage, soft humid soil, and insects impede his progress. "Encounters" with hitherto unknown animals, such as boa constricting snakes, and alligators, killed many of his party. Also, less than receptive natives took their toll; 14 of his crew were killed in one incident alone, when one of their canoes was attacked.

Mangrove area, a common ecosystem of the coast of Ecuador and northern Peru

Luckily, Ruiz returned, as did Almagro, with new military recruits from Panama who had recently arrived from Spain, burning with the desire to make their fortunes.

Both ships then proceeded south, and the thick mangrove swamps gave way to forests of ebony, mahogany, and sandlewood, interspersed with broad patches of cultivated land; cocoa in the low-lands, and maize and potato on the lush hillsides.

The villages became larger and more numerous as well. At Ta-camez in present day Ecuador, the Spanish observed a town of over 2000 houses, laid out in a system of streets. The people, both men and women, were frequently adorned with jewelery of gold and precious stones, especially emeralds.

However, once again the Spanish were not warmly received. A group of canoes, filled with warriors, intercepted the two ships, making menacing gestures. Meanwhile, a small shore party, which had arrived on the beach before the major tension erupted, had their

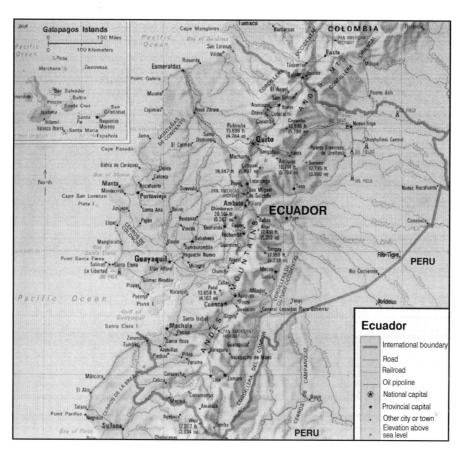

Map of present-day Ecuador

lives spared due to a mishap whereby one of the Spanish horsemen fell from his mount. This so shocked the natives that they temporarily withdrew, because they thought that the horse and rider were one being.

Many of Pizarro's crew wanted to return to Panama, as they were afraid that the farther south they went, the more numerous the natives would become, and the more hostile.

Defiant as always, Pizarro refused to give up or give in. He convinced some of his men to stay with him on the small island of Gallo; almost unpopulated and far enough away from the mainland that attack from natives from the mainland was unlikely.

Almagro guided both of the ships back to Panama, to re-supply and recruit more men. However, news leaked out from some of the returning crew of the appalling conditions that Pizarro had forced his fellow Spaniards to undergo, and upon hearing this the governor refused to give further assistance to Pizarro.

After gentle coaxing from Almagro and Luque, the governor consented to allowing a small provisioned ship to return and pick up Pizarro and his crew. From there he was given a maximum of six months to continue his exploration, and then return to Panama, no matter what.

They set off, and the two natives from Tumbes (the ones from the balsa craft) guided them south. After approximately three weeks, the ship lay anchor off the island of Santa Clara, at the entrance to Tumbes.

The next morning Pizarro beheld Tumbes, a town of considerable size, where many of the buildings were made of stone and plaster. A large flotilla of balsa crafts were also sighted; a war party about to depart and engage their enemies on the nearby island of Puna, according to the two natives on board.

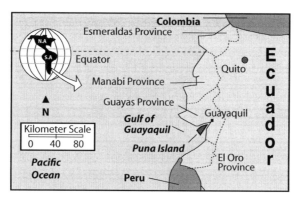

Map showing location of Puna Island

Running alongside the balsa crafts, Pizarro invited the chiefs on board, and through the two Tumbes natives, asked for provisions of food, so that the Spanish could be refreshed, and thereby enter into friendly dialogue with the leaders of the native town.

At this time, there happened to be an Incan nobleman, or Orejon in Tumbes, and he accompanied the food supply raft. Pizarro greeted him gracefully, and explained through the interpreters, the mysteries and wonders of the European ship.

The Peruvian chief was especially desirous to know from where Spanish had come, and why they were there. Pizarro replied that he had been sent by a great prince, the greatest and most powerful in the world, and that this prince had sent him to this country to claim lawful supremacy over it. Also, he had come to rescue the chief and all of his people from their dark beliefs, and give them the knowledge of the one true God, Jesus Christ.

The Indian chief listened with deep attention, but did not answer Pizarro. It may be that the interpreters did not know who Jesus was, or that there could not possibly be any king or chief superior to the Sapa Inca. But, whatever the reason, he maintained a discreet silence.

He remained on board for dinner, and thoroughly enjoyed the strange dishes and wine which he was offered. On taking his leave, he invited the Spanish to visit Tumbes, and was given, amongst other gifts, an iron hatchet, which he greatly admired, as the use of iron was not a material common in the Tahuantinsuyu.

The next day, Pizarro sent one of his men, Alonso de Molina ashore, accompanied by an African member of his crew, who had joined the vessel in Panama. They took with them gifts of pigs and wine, both of which were foreign to the New World. Molina was escorted to the residence of the Inca Orejon, which was quite lavish, including many plates and vessels of gold and silver from which the Inca was served. Later on, he was escorted about the city, and what really caught his eye was the temple, blazing with gold and silver decorations. Disbelieving Molinas account, Pizarro decided to send a different and more discreet emissary the next day; in essence, a spy.

Pedro de Candia was chosen. Dressed in metal armour, he attracted even more attention than Molinas and the African sailor. He was shown the same places that the earlier two had seen, including the temple. Upon his return to the ship, he was able to corroborate that the temple was literally tapestried with plates of gold and silver. Moreover, he saw the gardens inside the convent of the "Virgins Of The Sun" located nearby, which glowed with realistic gold and silver fruits and vegetables.

Pizarro and the other Spaniards were nearly mad with joy, knowing that their dreams of finding the mythical El Dorado had been realized. Having now all of the information he needed to fulfill his objective, Pizarro sailed south, in order to further explore the coast, for the capital city, whose name and location he had not yet discovered, was yet to be found.

His next stop was the port of Payta, Ecuador, where he was warmly received by the inhabitants. Once again he was greeted with balsa crafts filled with fruits, fish, and vegetables. This welcome was met at other locales as he continued south.

The soldier and conqueror Pizarro had not yet shown himself yet in his true colours, for he was too weak to do so.

In each of the ports of call, Pizarro heard the same accounts from the natives of a powerful central monarch who ruled over all the land that he had visited, and beyond. He was told that this Sapa Inca lived in the central mountains of the interior, where his capital shone with gold and silver.

Little gold was acquired on this leg of the second voyage, for most of it was held and used by the religious authorities in the larger settlements, and housed in the central temples.

He sailed as far south as present-day Trujillo. As he deemed that his military force was not strong enough to conquer even the towns that he had already visited, it seemed prudent to return to Panama, and enlist as many men and armaments as possible in order to achieve his primary goal; conquest of the Inca Empire.

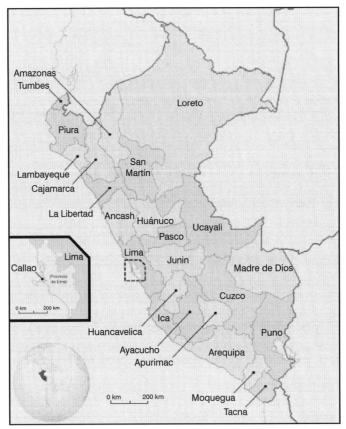

Map of Peru with border designations of present-day departments

At Tumbes, some of his crew wished to stay ashore with the natives. Pizarro complied with their request, hoping upon his return, that these Spaniards would have learned enough of the native language and customs to assist him in his goals.

He also acquired 3 natives, and one of them, named by the Spaniards "Felipillo" was to play a very important role in future events.

UNA BREVE HISTORIA DE LOS INCAS

Upon reaching Panama, which he had not seen for 18 months, Pizarro was given a hero's welcome. This is perhaps due to the fact that most of the inhabitants thought that he had surely perished, having sailed off into the distance, into uncharted waters.

Luque and the others that had financed him were especially joyous, for now they felt that their investments had been, or soon would be, repaid many times over. The governor, Rios, however, was less than enthusiastic. When Luque and the other associates pressed him for patronage of the third expedition, which they figured would cost more than they could raise, he coldly replied "He had no desire to build up other states at the expense of his own; nor would he be led to throw away any more lives than had already been sacrificed by the cheap display of gold and silver toys and a few Peruvian sheep".

Luque suggested that the only entity with funds enough to finance the third expedition would be the crown itself, in Spain. Pizarro was selected to be the best one to plead their case, as he had been, after all, in charge of both previous expeditions, and was quite an elegant and forceful speaker. In the spring of 1528, he sailed for Spain, along with Pedro de Candia, some of the natives, a few llama, cloth fabrics, ornaments of gold and silver, and his wonderful story.

The crossing from Panama to Spain was swift and uneventful, and Pizarro arrived in Seville in the summer of 1528. Immediately upon arrival, he was arrested for unpaid debts incurred earlier on, and put in prison. Pizarro, who had left Spain a forlorn and homeless adventurer, and after a twenty year absence, found himself a captive of the crown.

However, once the Court had heard of his arrival and the great purpose of his mission, he was immediately released. He was warmly received by the Emperor Charles The Fifth, in Toledo. Charles was intrigued by the llamas that Pizarro showed off, and the exquisite fabrics that had been made from its wool, but more than anything, it was the gold that caught his attention.

Pizarro's story of his adventures and travails endured in the New World, on behalf of the Crown, intrigued not only the Emperor, but all who heard it, for not only was Pizarro a natural actor, but he also knew that this presentation would affect his future fortunes. Charles recommended that he receive whatever funds and resources were required, within reason, to fulfill a successful third expedition, and on July 26, 1529, the required documents were signed.

The document, called the "capitulation", secured for Pizarro the right of discovery and conquest of Peru, or New Castile as it was then called. He was to receive the titles of Governor and Captain-general of the province, with a good salary, and Almagro was declared commander of the fortress at Tumbes. Luque was not left out; he became Bishop of Tumbes, and Protector Of The Indians Of Peru.

Pizarro was instructed to, within six months of signing the contract, raising a force of 250 men; 100 from the colonies, and the Crown would provide some funding for the purchase of artillery and other weapons. Finally, he was to be prepared, no later than 6 months of arriving in Panama, of commencing his expedition.

From Toledo, Pizarro visited his birthplace, Trujillo. There, he recruited old friends, who were mesmerized by his tales, and wished to participate in this once in a lifetime adventure. Four of his brothers also chose to join him; Francisco Martin de Alcantara (from his mother's side of the family), and Gonzalo, Juan, and Hernando Pizarro.

The stipulated 6 months passed, and although he was not able to assemble the complete complement of men required, he secured 3 small ships and with what provisions he had, set sail from Seville. Upon reaching Panama after an uneventful voyage, he had trouble recruiting colonists, as most had heard, in grim detail, of the problems and hardships encountered on the two previous adventures.

In the end, he had a crew of 180 men, and 27 horses. The three ships used for the Atlantic crossing were replaced with three on the

Pacific side, and in July of 1531 he set sail on his third, and last voyage to Peru. The weather was unfavourable, and instead of landing in Tumbes, he was forced to disembark near the Bay Of St. Matthew, to the north, while the ships continued hugging the coast southwards.

After a difficult march through streams and estuaries, they reached a small village or town in the province of Coaque. The Spanish rushed in, and as the frightened natives fled into the nearby forests, the Spanish pillaged the dwellings. They were amazed at the quantity of crude but large gold objects they found, as well as emeralds, some as large as pigeon's eggs. All of these spoils were deposited in a common heap, and after the required one fifth for the Crown was set aside, the remainder was divided amongst the present crew.

The ships returned, and the Crown's portion, as well as most of the rest of the booty was placed on board, to be taken back to Panama. Pizarro wagered that the ships' quick return to Panama, with such a display of wealth, would surely attract enough attention to attract more recruits. His gamble paid off in the end.

With the ships gone, Pizarro continued on foot, through sandy soil and intense burning sun. Progress was very slow, but these discomforts were nothing compared to a strange sickness that overcame many in his party. The main symptom was the formation of multiple and massive warts and blisters on their skin, which could lead to lethargy and death within 24 hours. This was probably small pox, and this was its introduction to Peru; a weapon, though not intentionally carried, that would prove far more lethal and devastating than any sword or rifle that the Spanish brought with them.

Word spread quickly amongst the native population, from village to village, that the foreigners, who had previously been gentle and friendly with them, had returned as ruthless destroyers.

The ship that had gone to Panama returned, and so Pizarro sailed with it to the island of Puna, near Tumbes, where he was warmly received by the natives there; enemies of the Inca who possibly now looked upon Pizarro as a possible ally in their resistance to Incan rule.

However, the two Tumben natives that had become part of Pizarro's crew felt that the Punans were setting a trap. Pizarro heeded the Tumbens' warning, and rounded up the 10 or 12 Punan chiefs present. At this time, having heard that the Spanish had returned, several Tumben warriors arrived, and the captured chiefs were promptly turned over to the Tumbens, who promtly executed them.

War immediately broke out between the Punans and Tumbens, with the Spanish taking the Tumben side. The weapons of the natives were not match for the Spaniards' Toledo steel swords and spears.

Two ships soon arrived to the island from Panama, bringing with them 100 volunteers and horses for the cavalry. With these reinforcements, Pizarro felt bold enough to cross over to the mainland and resume his military campaign, and the conquest of the Inca.

From the indians in Tumbes, he learned that the Tahuantinsuyu had been embroiled for some time in a civil war between two sons of the great Inca monarch, who had recently died. The two sons were battling each other for his throne.

This civil war was to become the pivotal event that allowed the Spanish to achieve their goal of conquest, for without the revolution that was dividing the entire Tahuantinsuyu, a handful of Spanish soldiers of fortune could never have prevailed over the military might of the largest civilization of the pre-Columbian Americas.

So let us step back in time, and see how this civil war came to be.

In the latter part of the fifteenth century, Sapa Inca Tupac Inca Yupanqui, the tenth Sapa Inca, had extended the Tahuantinsuyu from present day Santiago de Chile in the south, to the provinces of Quito,

Ecuador to the north. The acquisition of the Quito territory was made by his son, Huayna Capac.

Spanish ink drawing depicting Huayna Capac

The first arrival of Europeans on the Pacific shores of South America occurred about 10 years prior to the death of Huayna Capac, when Balboa crossed over from the Atlantic side of Panama. It is doubtful that Huayna Capac would have heard about this first appearance However, Pizarro and Almagro's first voyage, which reached the populated Rio de San Juan, was probably brought to the attention of Incan officials, if not the Sapa Inca himself, as this area was within the influence of the Tahuantinsuyu.

Some popular accounts state that supernatural appearances occurred at the time of, or prior to the arrival of the Spanish. Comets were seen in the heavens; earthquakes shook the land; the moon was encircled with rings of multi-coloured fire; a thunderbolt fell on one of the royal palaces and burned it to the ground; and an eagle, chased by several hawks, was seen hovering in the air above the Plaza de

Armas in Cuzco. The hawks attacked and killed the eagle, an event reportedly witnessed by a number of Inca, who interpreted it as the death of themselves.

It is probable that witnessed accounts of the arrival of strange, white coloured and bearded men, from early on, would have aroused attention amongst the native people, and word would have spread, if gradually. However, once any information or appearance reached the Tahuantinsuyu, the efficient Chasquis and Incan road system would have ensured that the Sapa Inca would be briefed in an expedited fashion.

The successor to Huayna Capac, as we have read, was Huascar, second son of his first wife and sister. The first son, Ninan Cuyochi, died of smallpox in 1527, and so the title and reponsibility of Sapa Inca was passed down to Huascar. Another son, whose role will become important later on, was Manco Capac, whose mother was the same as Huascar. However, the most beloved son of Huayna Capac was Atahuallpa, of Incan blood on his father's side, and of the royal Scyri blood of Quito on his mother's.

Spanish ink drawing of Huascar

Huayna Capac's last years were spent in Quito, not Cuzco, and Atahuallpa was his constant companion. Such was the love from father to son that Huayna Capac broke with the tradition of all of the Sapa Inca before him, and decided to divide the Tahuantinsuyu between Huascar and Atahuallpa.

On his deathbed, calling all of the great officials to him, Huayna Capac declared that Atahuallpa should inherit the ancient kingdom of Quito, as it was the dominion of his ancestors, and the rest belonged to Huascar.

His death, it is believed took place at the end of 1525, not quite 7 years before Pizarro`s arrival at Puna. His heart was kept in Quito, and the rest of his body was embalmed, and moved to the Coricancha in Cuzco, to lie with the mummified remains of his ancestors.

For nearly 5 years after the death of Huayna Capac, relative peace seemed to exist between the two brothers.

In character, Huascar seemed the more gentle and level-headed of the two brothers. Atahuallpa, on the other hand, was of a fiery temper, and began to test the boundary between the two kingdoms. The exact nature or territorial area that created initial friction is unclear, however, what we know is that war broke out in the border area of the two kingdoms, and Atahuallpa was defeated and made prisoner by Huascar`s troops near Tumebamba. This was a favourite residence of their father, in the territory of Quito and in the district of Canaris. He was able to escape, and upon his arrival back on home territory, found himself the head of a huge and experienced army, because many of the best soldiers and military heads lived in Quito, protectors of Huayna Capac. Allegiance of this army naturally passed down to Atahuallpa, and he had two of the Tahuantinsuyu`s finest commanders at his disposal; one was named Quiz-quiz, and the other, who was his maternal uncle, was Chullcuchima.

Early Spanish drawing depicting Atahuallpa

UNA BREVE HISTORIA DE LOS INCAS

Atahuallpa marched south, and by the time he reached Ambato, about 60 miles south of Quito, clashed with the armies of Huascar, moving north. After a day of hard fighting, Atahuallpa rose triumphant. From here he moved on to Tumebamba, where the Canaris people, with allegiance to Huascar, were slaughtered, and the city burned to the ground.

He advanced towards Cajamarca, where he halted with a detachment of the army. The main body of his forces, under his two generals, was to continue on to Cuzco. Atahuallpa chose to hold back in Cajamarca, because if he was to venture further into the enemies' territory, and be defeated, he would certainly be captured and killed. Also, this made Cajamarca a base, from which to re-enforce his generals, if need be, or beat a hasty retreat back to Quito.

His two generals advanced rapidly, crossing the Apurimac River and were soon closing in on Cuzco. However, Huascar had not been idle. Upon hearing of the defeat of his army at Ambato, he did everything in his power to raise troops and taxes throughout the Tahuantinsuyu.

Contrary perhaps, to common military logic, Huascar, on the advice of his priests, waited until Atahuallpa's troops were a few miles from Cuzco, and then he set out to do battle.

The two armies met on the plains of Quipaypan, on the outskirts of Cuzco. Whether one side or the other had an advantage in terms of troop strength, Atahuallpa's army were more experienced and disciplined, because Huascar's troops had been hastily collected, using any fit male that could be found. But, both fought as if they had everything at stake; because they did. This was no longer a border skirmish, but a battle for control of the entire Tahuantinsuyu.

The warfare raged from sunrise to sunset, the ground littered with the dead and dying. At length, Atahuallpa's forces took the upper hand. Huascar's soldiers gave way in all directions, with the conqueror's forces in hot pursuit. With 1000 of his troops encircling to protect Huascar, Atahuallpa's army slashed through them to get to the Sapa Inca.

He was taken prisoner, and the victorious troops of Atahuallpa marched Huascar through the streets of Cuzco.

These events happened in the spring of 1532, a few months before the arrival of the Spanish. The news of his victory and capture of his half-brother soon reached Atahuallpa in Cajamarca. He gave orders that Huascar was to be treated with all of the respect due his social status, but that he should be moved to the stronghold of Xauxa (in the mountains east of present-day Lima) and held there in strict confinement.

After this, Atahuallpa invited all of the Incas throughout the Tahuantinsuyu to assemble in Cuzco, in order to figure out the best way to partition the Tahuantinsuyu between him and his brother. When all had arrived in the capital, they were surrounded by Atahuallpa's soldiers and butchered without mercy. His motive was to exterminate the entire Inca family, for each of them held a higher right to the throne, based on bloodline, than he did.

Now we return to Pizarro and his men on the island of Puna.

Upon landing on the shores of Tumbes, he found it in complete ruin, and the temple ransacked of its gold and other treasures. The natives there could not give a good explanation; some said that warfare between the Punans and Tumbens had caused it, while others blamed a mysterious plague that had arrived and caused social chaos.

He decided to divide the landing party; the bulk of his troops, into three parts. Those that were physically under the weather were to stay in Tumbes and form a base camp; he would venture south, and Hernando de Soto with a small retinue, was to explore the outskirts of the vast sierra, to the east. This was in early may, 1532.

On his journey south, he met up with little opposition. Farther along the coast, he established his first permanent settlement; present-day Piura. He collected up all of the gold and other spoils that he and his group had collected thus far on this third expedition, and had the metals melted down. Then he put it on board the three small ships, and sent them back to Panama, in order to pay back debts incurred for the provisioning of the vessels, and to entice more conscripts to the mission at hand.

During this journey, he learned from the natives of the struggle between the Inca brothers, and that the victor was now with his army encamped at a distance of only 10 or 12 days from Piura.

Pizarro hoped that the ships would return soon, so that he could begin moving inland, in pursuit of his quest to find the El Dorado that he had sought so desperately these many years. However, after several weeks, no reinforcements arrived. Yet, the longer he waited, the more his small group became restless, and might start to fracture.

With a total of 177 men, and 67 horses, he decided that the best course of action was to meet with Atahuallpa face to face. If he displayed himself as a peaceful representative of a brother monarch, he thought, he could dispel any feelings of hostility or suspicion that the Inca might hold. After this, he could regulate his future, based on the circumstances that presented themselves.

On september 24, 1532, five months after landing in Tumbes, Pizarro led his group out of Piura, having told the 50 soldiers that he left behind to treat the local natives with humanity, and conduct themselves in such a way as to promote good will with the surrounding tribes; their survival depended on it.

After crossing the smooth waters of the Piura river, the small army marched south, through forests and agricultural lands fed by canals and aqueducts. This was clearly an easier route than the mire of mangrove swamps that he had encountered earlier, on the two previous expeditions.

The natives that they encountered were gentle in nature, and provided them with food and lodging as they travelled; each of the Spanish deported themselves in an unthreatening way so as not to raise suspicion or un-needed conflict so early in their campaign.

On the fifth day, while camping in a lush cultivated valley, he called all of his men together, and told them that "a crisis had now arrived in their affairs, which it demanded all their courage to meet. No man should think of going forward in the expedition who could not do so with his whole heart, or who had the least misgiving as to its success. If any repented in his share of it, it was not too late to turn back. Piura was but poorly garrisoned, and he should be glad to see it in greater strength. Those that chose might return to this place, and they should be entitled to the same proportion of lands and indian vassals as the present residents. With the rest, were they few or many, who chose to take their chances with them, he should pursue the adventure to the end".

This was a clever tactic to use. If a man chose to stay on the quest, Pizarro knew that he was focussed and eager (and hopefully fit); if he chose to turn back, he would reinforce the fledgling colony of Piura. In all, 9 turned back; 4 infantrymen, and 5 cavalry.

On the second day of the renewed march, Pizarro and his men arrived at a native town called Zaran, where they were greeted warmly by the Curaca (Inca noble). The troops were housed in a Tambo or inn, for Zaran was located on one of the Incan roads. Here Pizarro learned that a garrison of Incan troops were stationed in a place called Caxas, a relatively short distance from them in the hills.

He immediately dispatched a small party under the head of Hernando de Soto to reconnoitre the ground, and bring back intelligence of the goings on at Caxas.

On the eighth morning, Soto returned, with an envoy of the Inca himself! He was clearly a person of rank, and was attended by several followers. He stated (through the two Tumben interpreters) that he had come to deliver a message from Atahuallpa, and had brought presents for Pizarro.

The gifts consisted of two model fountains, made of stone, resembling fortresses, woollen garments embroidered with gold and silver, and perfume made from pulverized and seasoned goose flesh. The ambassador also stated that Atahuallpa welcomed the strangers to his country, and invited them to visit with him in his camp in the mountains.

Pizarro well understood that the Inca's objective was that the ambassador glean as much information as possible as to the numbers and weaponry of the Spanish. He implored that the ambassador stay with them for some days, yet the latter declined. With gifts for the Inca of a crimson cloth cap, some cheap but flashy glass ornaments, and other trinkets, Pizarro told the envoy to tell Atahuallpa that the Spanish had come from a powerful prince who lived far away. He also said that they had learned of Atahuallpa's great victories, and had come to pay their respects to him. They had come to offer their services of aiding him with their arms against his enemies, and were eager to meet with him at his earliest convenience.

Pizarro then received from De Soto a full account of his expedition. He stated that upon entering Caxas, he was met with armed opposition, but upon stating pacific intentions, was met with courtesy. A royal Incan officer told him that Atahuallpa was in Cajamarca, with a large army, enjoying the natural hot springs that this place was, and still is, famous for. He was also able to ascertain details of the the resources and general policies of the Sapa Inca's government.

From Caxas, De Soto travelled to the adjacent town of Guancabamba, which was larger and more refinely built than Caxas.

Instead of the houses being made of sun-baked clay, many were constructed of solid stone, with the near-perfect joinery that was to make Incan architecture famous. One of the great Inca roads also passed though the town, with Tambos (inns) located at an even space of 5 to 10 miles.

Fine example of few remaining sections of the Incan road system

Pizarro sent word back to Piura of his location and present condition, and then resumed his march, taking a route south. He chose not to follow the Incan road, as this could make him vulnerable to attack.

Hernando Pizarro was sent forward, and, upon reaching a group of indians, interrogated one as regards the Sapa Inca. Refusing to answer his questions, Hernando tortured him until he spoke. The native said that Atahuallpa was camped with three separate divisions of infantry, and was aware of the approach of the Spanish, and their small number. Also, Atahuallpa was purposely decoying them towards his present location, in order to have them more completely in his power.

This account caused Pizarro much anxiety. He instructed one of his native interpreters to go as a spy into the Inca's quarters, and learn of Atahuallpa`s intentions towards the Spaniards. He was to inform the Inca of the uniformly considerate way that he and his men had treated the natives along their journey, and to assure him that they were now coming in full confidence of finding him with the same amicable feelings towards themselves. Also, the interpreter was to observe if the Inca road on which he would be travelling was being defended, or if any preparations of a hostile nature could be discerned.

With this, Pizarro continued his march, and after 3 days, found himself at the base of the mountain rampart behind which lay Cajamarca.

This was a pivotal moment in the conquest, and in order to bolster the spirit of the troops, Pizarro made a speech in order to strengthen their resolve. "Let every one of you, take heart and go forward like a good soldier, nothing daunted by the smallness of your numbers. For in the greatest extremity God ever fights for his own; and doubt not He will humble the pride of the heathen, and bring him to the knowledge of the true faith, the great end and object of the Conquest".

That night Pizarro held council with his principle officers. It was decided that he should lead advance, with forty cavalry and sixty infantry; the rest, under Hernando, would remain where they were, until further orders were given.

At dawn the small party embarked on the Inca road, which drove deep and high into the mountains. The road was of excellent condition, but was so steep that the cavalry had to dismount in order to keep moving forward. After all, the Inca architects had not designed the grade of the road for horses, but for the sure-footed Chasquis and trains of llama.

Late in the afternoon Pizarro sent a few of his troops back to tell Hernando to proceed forward, as they had advanced without opposition. As night fell, Pizarro and his men camped out in a deserted fortress.

The next day he continued on, rising higher and higher into the mountains. The rich vegetation of the lower altitudes gave way to thin pine forests, and then to the yellow grass of the altiplano. The cold was severe, and especially affected the horses. Here Pizarro made camp, waiting for his brother to join them.

They had not been long in these quarters when an envoy arrived, with a message from Atahuallpa. Pizarro was informed that the Incan road was free of enemies, and that an embassy was presently on its way from the Inca to the Spanish camp. Pizarro then sent his own messengers back along the road, in order to quicken Hernando's arrival, because he did not want the Inca to be informed of his diminished numbers.

Hernando and his group showed up just before that of the Inca's ambassadors, with the latter offering gifts of llamas to the Spanish commander. The leader of the Peruvian contingent also brought greetings from his master, who wished to know when the Spanish planned to reach Cajamarca, so that he might provide them with refreshments.

As the ambassador spoke in lofty terms of the military prowess and resources of Atahuallpa, Pizarro pretended not to be impressed. He agreed that Atahuallpa's triumphs had indeed been impressive, but that the Spaniards' monarch was far more powerful. This was clearly evident, he suggested, from the ease with which the Spanish had overrun any native nation that they had previously encountered. He had indeed been led to his present situation based on accounts he had heard of Atahuallpa's triumphs (or so he said) and wished to offer his services in the Inca's wars, if he were to be received in a cordial and friendly manner. In fact, he was prepared to postpone his original plan to journey to the opposite seas, for a while, if this pleased the Inca.

According to the Spanish accounts of this encounter, the ambassador was awed by what Pizarro had said. More likely though, he saw it for what it was; the bragging of a foreigner, whose ambitions were more than diplomatic.

For the next two days, Pizarro and his men marched through the icy air of the altiplano. Upon beginning their descent on the eastern side of the mountains, they were met by another emissary from Atahuallpa, who again offered a gift of llamas. This time, however, he was drinking Chicha, the fermented drink made of maize, offered in golden goblets known as Qeros.

A pure gold Qero; the drinking vessel containing Chicha, or corn beer drunk by nobility

After a short meeting, the ambassador withdrew, and Pizarro continued his descent. After three days they arrived in view of the valley of Cajamarca.

The white houses of the city shone in the sun, surrounded by verdant hills. Beyond Cajamarca, white clouds of steam rose, showing the location of the famous hot springs, and along the nearby hillsides, glittering like a large cluster of diamonds on a green background, were the pavilions of the Incan Army.

"It filled us all with amazement", explained one of the Spanish soldiers, "to behold the Indians occupying such a proud position. So many tents, so well appointed, as were never seen in the Indies till now. The spectacle caused something like confusion and even fear in the stoutest bosom. But it was too late to turn back, or to betray the least sign of weakness, since the natives in our own company would, in such case, have been the first to rise upon us. So, with as bold a countenance as we could, after coolly surveying the ground, we prepared for our entrance into Cajamarca".

Pizarro formed his little army into three groups, and moved forward, at a leisurely pace, down the slopes that led to Cajamarca.

It was late in the afternoon of november 15, 1532 when he entered the city. They found Cajamarca completely deserted. The only sound that the Spanish heard was he sound of their horses hooves on the hard ground.

The weather, which had been fine earlier in the day, turned cloudy, and rain mixed with hail began to fall. Pizarro was so anxious to find out about the disposition of the Inca that he sent Hernando de Soto, with 15 cavalry, in the direction of Atahuallpa's camp. Immediately after de Soto's departure, Pizarro sent his brother Hernando and twenty additional troops to bolster the strength of the party.

De Soto and Hernando soon came to a broad but narrow stream, and on the other side stood a battalion of Inca warriors. The Spanish carefully but purposefully forded the stream, with the indian warriors offering no opposition; in fact, one of them pointed out the location of Atahuallpa.

The great Inca was seated on a cushion in an open courtyard, surrounded by his nobles and officials, all dressed in bright opulent attire. Atahuallpa was not as ornately dressed, but wore on his head the red crimson fringe, or Borla, that only a Sapa Inca was allowed to use; a right that he claimed after the capture of his brother Huascar.

Hernando Pizarro and de Soto, with two or three of their men, slowly rode up in front of the Inca, and Hernando Pizarro, being respectful but not dismounting, told Atahuallpa that he came as an ambassador of his brother, the commander of the white men, to inform him of their arrival in Cajamarca. He continued by saying that they were the subjects of a mighty prince from across the waters, and that they were there to offer their services to the Inca. In addition, Atahuallpa was invited to visit with his brother in their present quarters, near the central square, in Cajamarca.

To this Atahuallpa did not answer a single word, nor even make the slightest gesture acknowledging that he had understood a single word spoken, even though, Felipillo, one of the natives present in the Spanish group, had clearly translated Hernando's message.

In a courteous and respectful manner, Hernando Pizarro broke the silence by requesting that the Inca speak to them himself, and inform them of his pleasure. To this Atahuallpa condescended to reply, with a slight smile on his lips, "Tell your captain that I am keeping a fast, which will end tomorrow morning. I will then visit him, with my chieftains. In the meantime, let him occupy the public buildings on the square, and no other, till I come, when I will order what shall be done".

De Soto, observing that Atahuallpa eyed his horse with some interest, immediately put on a show of his horsemanship, and the well trained instincts of his mount. He then charged towards the Inca, and at the last moment rose the horse on his haunches. Some of the foam from the horses' mouth struck Atahuallpa's garments, but he did not flinch, showing the same cool composure and stony face that had been present through the entire interview.

Refreshments were offered by the Inca's entourage, which the Spanish declined, being unwilling to dismount. They did, however, accept the offer of Chicha presented to them in large gold Qeros.

After taking a respectful leave of the Inca, the Spanish rode back to Cajamarca, their minds swirling with doubts. They had seen the strength of his military, or at least a portion of it, and contrasted that with their diminutive force.

The valley of Cajamarca

Upon reaching camp, their glum mood started to infect the other Spaniards, which grew as night fell, for they could see the watch-fires of the Peruvians lighting up the sides of the mountains, "as thick", one said "as the stars of heaven".

The only one in the camp with bright spirits was, as always, Pizarro. He knew that he had to immediately boost the moral of the others, or all would be lost. In a forceful statement he announced (that

76   UNA BREVE HISTORIA DE LOS INCAS

"they were to rely on themselves, and on that Providence which had carried them safe through so many fearful trials. It would not now desert them; and if numbers, however great, were on the side of their enemy, it mattered little, when the arm of Heaven was on theirs".

Such bold speeches, as he used effectively in times of peril and anguish in the past, worked once more.

He then summoned a council of his officers, in order to form a plan of action, or, more correctly, to propose to them a course of action that he had already formulated himself. This was to ambush Atahuallpa and take him prisoner in front of the whole Incan army

What sounds like a rash and even insane proposal, was probably the only choice that the Spanish felt that they had. To retreat was impossible; if they attempted this, the whole army of the Inca would be upon them. The roads would be occupied and blocked, and they would be hemmed in on all sides.

Also, to remain inactive for long would probably be equally as perilous. Their seemingly magical horses and weaponry would soon lose any sense of supernatural wonder once the Inca became familiar with them, and their diminutive numbers would then show their true value; little in comparison to the sheer size and physical fighting skills of the Inca's army.

Their fear of the Inca's retribution may seem like paranoia to some, but, due to his rather stealthy character, and blank expressions, the Spanish could still not figure out Atahuallpa's intentions towards them. What they believed now, was that he had ensnared them in a trap for which there was only one way out.

There was no time to be lost; they had learned that any day now his other forces, who had recently been victorious in the taking of Cuzco, would return north to re-group, making the Spanish forces look even smaller in comparison. However, to try and take Atahuallpa on the open field would be impossible, thus, the invitation that the Spanish had made for him to visit them in their quarters afforded them the best opportunity to abduct him.

Pizarro felt that by formulating a well-coordinated strategic plan, with each man having an important and specific role, their small number could actually be advantageous. But, it would clearly be advantageous if the Inca were to arrive with a small contingent, rather than the whole army. Once secured, Pizarro theorized, Atahuallpa's followers, shocked by this turn of events, would withdraw out of bewilderment, and then, with the Inca subdued, Pizarro could dictate laws to him, and thus the entire Tahuantinsuyu.

Pizarro based this rather unorthodox plan on the exploits of Cortez, who had used similar techniques to capture Monteczuma of the Aztecs in Mexico, and in the end crush that civilization.

The cloudy and rainy weather of the previous day gave way to bright sunshine of a new morning, the sixteenth of november, 1532. The loud cry of a trumpet called the Spaniards to arms that morning, and Pizarro, briefly acquainting them with his bold plan, prepared for what would be the most important and decisive day of his life.

The plaza, in which they camped, was triangular in shape, with low buildings, or halls, on all three sides. Into these he stationed the cavalry in two divisions, one under his brother Hernando, and the other de Soto. The infantry were placed in another of these buildings, with 20 being served for Pizarro's use as a contingency force. Another of Pizarro's men, Pedro de Candia, with a few men and two falconets (small canons) set themselves up in the nearby Incan stone fortress.

All were instructed to remain at their posts until the arrival of Atahuallpa. Even after the Inca had entered the plaza, they were to remain quiet and hidden, until they heard the sound of a single gunshot. Then, in concert, they were to attack and slay the Peruvian soldiers, working their way as fast as possible to Atahuallpa.

It was late in the morning before any movement was visible in the Peruvian camp, where great preparations were being made, with pomp and ceremony, for the meeting of these two leaders. A message came from Ahatuallpa, that he was bringing with him fully-armed warriors, as Pizarro had done so the night before.

Pizarro had no reason to be surprised at this announcement, and to object would display a degree of distrust. Therefore, he expressed his satisfaction at this news, and assured Atahuallpa that he would be welcomed as a friend and brother.

About noon, the Incan procession began to move towards Cajamarca. In front came a large group of attendants, whose primary role seemed to be to sweep away every particle of rubbish from the road. High above all the others was Atahuallpa, carried aloft by his principle nobles, while others of the same rank flanked the royal litter, adorned with so much gold that they seemed to "blaze like the sun", according to one of the Spaniards. The rest of the entourage, the soldiers, were spread out on either side of the road as far as the eye could see.

When the royal procession had reached within half a mile of the city, it came to an abrupt halt; and Pizarro saw that Atahuallpa was preparing to pitch his tents, as if to set up camp there. A messenger soon arrived, telling the Spanish commander that the Inca planned to occupy his present position for the night, and arrive in Cajamarca early the next morning.

This frightened Pizarro, as his men were all on guard, including the mounted cavalry, and ready for battle at any moment. To delay the conflict until the next day might prove disastrous, for by then they would all be tired, and their nervous edge would be gone; the tight wound-up spring of the Spanish warrior would be loose and limp.

In response to Atahuallpa's message, Pizarro told the messenger to tell the Inca of his deep disappointment, as he had already organized everything for his entertainment, and had expected that Atahuallpa would dine with him that evening.

Upon receiving this information, the Inca immediately broke camp, and began his march to Cajamarca, leaving the majority of his soldiers behind, being accompanied by only few, who were unarmed. It is confusing that such a bold and supposedly ruthless leader as Atahuallpa would venture into the camp of a foreign unknown unarmed. Most researchers believe that he truly trusted Pizarro and his words of friendship, and therefore chose to visit the Spaniards in a manner that implied entire confidence in their good faith.

As supreme commander of the military, head of state, and descendant of the sun (on his father's side, at least) he perhaps felt that no earthly power could harm him, however, he clearly did not know the character of the foreigners who now lay in wait for him.

Just before sunset, the royal procession entered the gates of the city. First came the hundreds of servants, who swept all rubbish and obstacles from the path. Next came people of different ranks, wearing either fancy clothes of red and white, like a chess board, or pure white, and bearing ceremonial hammers and maces made of copper and silver. The guards, who were in the direct vicinity of Atahuallpa, wore rich blue garments, and were adorned with ornaments of gold.

Elevated high above all of the others was Atahuallpa, seated on an open litter (throne) of gold, draped with richly coloured tapestries depicting tropical birds, and studded with burnished sheets of gold and silver. His attire on this occasion was much richer than on the preceding evening. Around his neck he wore a collar of large emeralds, and his short black hair was adorned with golden ornaments, as well as the scarlet Borla, which encircled his temples.

As the leading files of the procession entered the square, they created an opening, to the left and right, for the royal litter to pass. It seemed as if the whole event had been orchestrated, so wonderful was its state of organization. once 5 or 6 thousand of his people had entered the plaza, Atahuallpa halted, and after an inquiring look around stated "where are the strangers?".

At this moment, Fray Vicente de Valverde, a Dominican friar, Pizarro's chaplain, came forward with his bible in one hand, and a crucifix in the other. Approaching the Inca, he told him, through Felipillo the interpreter, that he had come by order of his commander to explain to Atahuallpa the doctrines of the "true" faith, for which purpose the Spaniards had come from a great distance to this country. The friar then explained, or at least tried to, the doctrine of the Trinity, the creation of man and his subsequent fall, the redemption of Jesus, and the passing on of the Saviour's message and church to Peter.

Next, he taught Atahuallpa about the Popes, who, as God's representatives on earth, held power over all leaders and people. One of these last popes, he stated, had commissioned the Spanish emperor, the mightiest monarch in the world, to conquer and convert the natives in this Western hemisphere, and to this purpose in Peru, had appointed Francisco Pizarro. The friar concluded with beseeching Atahuallpa to receive Pizarro kindly, to confess the errors of his own faith, and to embrace Jesus; the only one who could offer him salvation. Furthermore, the Inca should (or must) acknowledge himself as a subject of Emperor Charles the Fifth, who would thereby aid and protect him.

It is hard to know if Atahuallpa was able to grasp all or even some of the concepts presented by the friar through Felipillo the interpreter, who probably only had a rudamentary knowledge of Christianity. For example, the great Spanish historian Garcilaso states, that Felipillo explained the Trinity by saying that "the Christians believed in three Gods and one God, and that made four". However, he probably got the gist of the presentation; resign your position, forget your Gods, and give Emperor Charles what he wants.

The eyes of the Inca flashed with fire, and his dark brow grew darker, as he replied, "I will be no man's tributary. I am greater than any Prince upon earth. Your emperor may be a great prince; I do not doubt it, when I see that he has sent his subjects so far across the waters; and I am willing to hold him as a brother. As of the Pope of whom you speak, he must be crazy to talk of giving away countries which do not belong to him. For my faith". He continued, "I will not change it. Your own God, as you say, was put to death by the very men whom he created. But mine". He concluded, pointing to the sun, slowly setting, "my God still lives in the heavens and looks down on his children".

He then demanded of Valverde by what authority he had said these things. The friar pointed to the book that he held, and Atahuallpa, taking it in his hands and briefly looking at a few pages, threw it on the ground and demanded, "Tell your comrades that they shall give me an account of their doings in my land. I shall not go from here till they have made me full satisfaction for all the wrongs they have committed".

The friar, fuming with rage at what had been done to his sacred text, bent over, picked it up, and made straight for Pizarro, saying "Do you not see that while we stand here wasting our breath in talking with this dog, full of pride as he is, the fields are filling with Indians? Set on at once, I absolve you".

Pizarro saw that his hour had come He waved a white scarf in the air, the appointed signal. With this, the single gunshot issued from the fortress. Then, the commander and his followers sprang into the square, shouting the war cry "St. Jago at them". This was echoed by the battle cry of every Spaniard in the city, and they poured into the plaza, cavalry and infantry, throwing themselves into the Indian crowd.

The Peruvians, taken by surprise, panicked. They were stunned by the sound of the muskets, blinded by the acrid smoke issuing from them, and choked of the sulphurous gas. The cavalry, horse and rider acting as a single unit of death, trampled them, noble and commoner alike, as the flash of swords cut through the muskets' fog, and through the flesh and bone of the helpless Peruvians.

The main avenue of escape was closed off; for the entrance to the plaza was now choked with the bodies of those to tried to escape the melee. The sheer pressure of the crowd on one section of the plaza's wall of stone and dried clay caused it to crumble, and as the multitudes attempted to flee across the nearby fields, they were cut down by the cavalry.

Meanwhile the fight, or more accurately put, the massacre, continued in a heated manner around the Inca. His faithful nobles, surrounding his litter, threw themselves against the horses, trying to unseat the riders by grabbing at their saddles, or acting as human shields, taking the sword thrusts that were destined for their leader. The fact that they did not strike back with weapons of their own proves that they didn't carry any, that day.

As one noble fell to the sword or was trampled underneath the hooves of a horse, another took his place. The Inca, stunned and bewildered, and seeing his faithful servants being cut down in numbers that he could not comprehend, held onto his seated place in the litter as best he could as it danced and rocked in the air. His feeling of helplessness at this moment must have been unfathomable.

As the shade of evening grew deeper, and weary of their day of unparalleled destruction, some of the Spaniards attempted to assault Atahuallpa directly, in order to bring the battle to a close. But Pizarro, who was standing next to the Inca, called out, "Let no one who values his life strike at the Inca", and stretching an arm out to shield him, received a wound on his hand from one of his own men; the only wound received by a Spaniard in the course of the events.

The struggle became fiercer around the royal litter, and with few of the nobles left unhurt (or dead) to hold it, the golden throne of the Sapa Inca toppled violently. Atahuallpa would have fallen hard on the stone pavement of the plaza were it not for Pizarro and some of his men who caught him in their arms. The royal Bola, symbol of his title as highest of all Inca, was immediately snatched from his temples by a soldier named Estele, and the Sapa Inca, fallen both physically and figuratively, was bound, and removed to a neighbouring building, where he was carefully guarded. All resistance by the Inca's forces

Fanciful Spanish depiction of the capture of Atahuallpa

abruptly stopped, and his fate soon spread throughout the Tahuan-tinsuyu. Without the Inca as top and center of all political, military, and religious activity and decision-making, the systems of the Tahuantin-suyu began to crumble from the top down.

Not only was the Sapa Inca now removed from the center of power, but with the death or injury of many of his nobles, many of the corresponding chains of command were also now broken.

Another Spanish pen and ink drawing of Atahuallpa's capture

Estimates of the number of Peruvians killed during the "battle" at Cajamarca vary, greatly. Pizarro's secretary recorded 2,000 deaths, while other accounts make it as high as 10,000. The true figure may never be known. Also, how could so few have killed so many? Well, for starters, the Peruvians, as we saw, came unarmed, as Pizarro told Ata-huallpa that he wished to welcome him as his "friend and brother".

"What wonder was it", reminisced one of the Inca nobles, "what wonder that our countrymen lost their wits, seeing blood run like water, and the Inca, we all of us adore, seized and carried off by a handful of men?"

That night, Pizarro dined with Atahuallpa. The banquet was held in one of the halls facing the plaza, which just hours ago had been the scene of the bloody attack, and was still strewn with the bodies of the Inca's subjects. Atahuallpa was seated next to his captor, and though he held the expression of someone who had still not fully grasped the full extent of the day's events, he showed amazing fortitude. "It is the fortune of war", he is reputed to have said.

During the dinner, he told Pizarro that he had been made acquainted of the progress of the Spanish from the hour of their landing, but that he had under-estimated their strength due to the smallness of their number. He never had any doubt that he could easily defeat them by the time they reached Cajamarca, but he had wanted them to cross over the mountains, unobstructed, in order to see what they were made of. By this, he could then choose those that he thought would be useful to him, gain possession of their mysterious weaponry and horses, and put the rest to death.

Pizarro paid every attention possible to his royal captive, and tried to lighten Atahuallpa's dour mood. He told him that his present position had been the lot of every Indian prince who had resisted the white man. He said that the Spanish had come into the country to proclaim the gospel of Jesus Christ, and that it was no wonder that they had prevailed, because the shield of the Saviour had protected them. "Heaven had permitted that Atahuallpa's pride should be humbled, because of his hostile intentions towards the Spaniards and the insult he had offered to the sacred volume". But he told the Inca to take courage and confide in him, for the Spanish were a generous race, warring only against those who made war on them, and showing grace to all who submitted.

Before retiring for the night, Pizarro briefly addressed his troops. Seeing that not one of them had been injured, he called them all to thank Providence for their miraculous victory, and he trusted that their lives had been thus protected and reserved for yet greater things. However, as they were now in the heart of the foes' kingdom, they must always be on their guard, and be prepared at any hour to be roused from their sleep by the call of the trumpet.

The next morning, Pizarro's first commands were to have the plaza cleaned, and the dead bodies buried. This was carried out by several Peruvians who had been captured the previous day. Also, he sent 30 of the cavalry to the Inca's quarters, out at the Peruvian army's camp, to collect all of the gold and silver objects and ornaments that it contained.

The cavalry party returned at about noon, with a large group of indians, men and women, many of the latter being the wives and attendants of Atahuallpa. The cavalry reported that they had not met with any resistance from the Incan forces that remained in the area. This is partly due to the fact that though large in number and able-bodied, the majority of the soldiers that Atahuallpa had at Cajamarca were younger and much less experienced than his main forces, which were still battling with those of Huascar near Cuzco.

The number of indian prisoners was so vast that some of the Spanish wanted them all put to death, or at least have their hands chopped off, so as to disable them from future acts against the conquerors. This gives some incite into the mentally that made up at least some of Pizarro's army The commander dismissed this idea at once, and dismissed the Peruvians back to their homes, with the assurance that none of them would be harmed in the future, as long as they didn't offer resistance to the white men.

Pizarro now turned his eyes towards the capital, Cuzco, but the distance was great, and his numbers small. In order to increase his numbers, he sent a courier back to Piura, to inquire if new recruits had recently arrived from Panama. While he awaited a response, he and his men set about building a church, and repairing some of the physical damage to the buildings that had been incurred in the recent fight.

It was not long before Atahuallpa discovered, amongst all of the show of religious zeal from the Spanish, an appetite much greater than those of religion or even ambition; that was their hunger for gold. This, he believed, could be the key to unlock the chains of his present predicament. Perhaps the Spanish would release him in exchange for a quantity of gold that would stagger their imaginations, more than they and their horses could possibly carry.

Pure gold Inca drinking vessels

There was also Huascar to contend with. Although he was imprisoned and heavily guarded at Andamarca, a relatively short

UNA BREVE HISTORIA DE LOS INCAS

distance from Cajamarca, upon hearing of Atahuallpa's own present condition, Huascar might bribe his guards, make his escape, and then present himself to Pizarro as the true Sapa Inca.

Thus, Atahuallpa told Pizarro that if he were to be set free, he would cover the floor of the apartment in which they presently stood with gold. Those present listened, and gently smiled, or possibly even smirked, because they knew, or at least dreamed, that such an offer was a pittance of what lay before them.

Since Pizarro did not immediately respond to his offer, Atahuallpa raised it, considerably. He stated that, "he would not merely cover the floor, but would fill the room with gold as high as he could reach". Pizarro accepted this offer, since by doing so he could collect all of the gold that would be promptly and easily available, and prevent it from being hidden or removed by the native populace.

The apartment was about 17 feet wide by 22 feet long, and the line that marked where Atahuallpa's fingers reached was about 9 feet from the floor. This would mean a volume of gold of 3366 cubic feet. However, the gold would not have to be melted into ingots first, it would fill the space based upon the shape and size of the articles that were collected. In addition, Atahuallpa agreed to fill an adjoining room of smaller dimension twice with silver, in like manner, requesting 2 months to carry out the task.

The apartment in Cajamarca in which Atahuallpa was held prisoner

He immediately dispatched couriers to Cuzco, and other principle centers in the Tahuantinsuyu, with orders that the gold ornaments and utensils be removed from all of the royal palaces, temples, and other public buildings, and be brought to Cajamarca without haste.

Meanwhile, he continued to live in quarters near the plaza, was treated with the respect due his rank, and provided with all of his needs, except freedom, of course. He walked about his apartmant unshackled, allowed the company of his favourite wives, and Pizarro ensured that his domestic privacy was not violated. His subjects had full access to him, and many visited, offering gifts, and condolences.

Huascar soon found out the situation that his half-brother and rival was in. In response, he attempted to get in contact with Pizarro,

90

offering a much higher ransom than Atahuallpa had, for his own release. After all, he wished to say, his half-brother had never dwelt in Cuzco, and therefore didn't know the quantity of treasure that Cuzco contained, nor where it was kept.

This intelligence was secretly communicated to Atahuallpa by one of Huascar's jailors, and the latter's rage was further fuelled by Pizarro's declaration that he intended to bring Huascar to Cajamarca, in order to fully understand the dispute between the two brothers. By this he would able to determine which of the two brothers would be best suited to be installed as Sapa Inca, and there after be the most effective pawn of the Spanish.

Atahuallpa was alarmed by Pizarro's desire to have the dispute between the two brothers brought before him, for he was afraid that the decision would go in favour of Huascar. He therefore decided that he had no choice but to have his-half-brother, and true heir to the Tahuantinsuyu killed.

His orders were immediately carried out, and Huascar was drowned, by Atahuallpa's agents, in the river of Andamarca. With his dying breath, Huascar declared that the white men would avenge his murder, and that his rival would not long survive him.

Atahuallpa received the news of his brother's demise with surprise and indignation. He immediately sent for Pizarro, and spoke of the event with the deepest expression of sorrow. The Spanish commander at first refused to believe the news, and bluntly told Atahuallpa that there was no way that Huascar could be dead, but, if any harm had indeed been done to him, Atahuallpa would answer for it.

To this the Inca replied that Huascar had indeed been killed, by his own keepers, who caught him trying to escape. Upon making further inquiries, Pizarro found that the reports were indeed true.

Several weeks had now passed since Atahuallpa's emissaries had been sent out to collect the gold and silver that would satisfy the ransom demands. But the distances were great, and the returns came in slowly. Most of the booty came as massive sheets of gold, weighing 50 to 75 pounds each. It was carried on the backs of porters, and upon reaching Cajamarca, were carefully registered, and placed under lock and key.

As the volume of the wealth began to amass, the Spanish grew impatient; they made no allowance for the distances covered by the porters, nor the difficulties of the terrain traversed. They even accused Atahuallpa of purposefully slowing the progress of the shipments, in order to buy more time. Rumours of an uprising by the Incan forces were beginning to circulate, and the Spanish were now afraid of a sudden assault on their quarters, and their acquired treasures.

After further inquiries, Pizarro found out that one of the places where the Indians were predicted to rendezvous was the neighbouring city of Huamachuco. Upon relaying this information to Atahuallpa, the latter indignantly replied, "No one of my subjects would dare to appear in arms, or raise his finger, without my orders. You have me in your power. Is not my life at your disposal? And what better security can you have for my fidelity?"

He then explained to Pizarro that the distances to which the porters had been travelling in order to acquire the ransom were, in many cases, very great. Cuzco, for example, could be reached by courier in five days or less, but the return trip, laden with gold, could take several weeks. "But that you may be satisfied I am proceeding in good faith, I desire you to send some of your own people to Cuzco. I will give them a safe conduct, and there, they can superintend the execution of the commission, and see with their own eyes that no hostile movements are intended". This seemed to be a fair offer, Pizarro thought, and it would also help him to learn more about the present state of affairs in Cuzco, and hopefully beyond.

Before sending emissaries on this trip to Cuzco, Pizarro dispatched his brother Hernando, with 20 horses and some infantry to Huamachuco, in order to see if the rumours of an uprising were true. Hernando found the town quiet, and was even kindly received by the natives. From there he travelled on to Pachacamac, a town situated on the coast, about 250 miles south of Cajamarca. This was the site of a massive temple complex consecrated and dedicated to Pachacamac, the Creator of the world, also known as the Lord of the Earthquake.

Hernando was informed by the natives that altars had existed on this site at the time of arrival of the first Peruvians, and so great was the veneration of this God and place by the locals that the Inca, instead of attempting to abolish His worship, found it more prudent to allow it to continue, conjointly with that of Inti, their supreme deity. The natives throughout the Tahuantinsuyu still made pilgrimages to this site, to commune with the Oracle that dwelt there, and pay tribute. This made Pachacamac one of the most opulent temples in the Tahuantinsuyu, and Atahuallpa, anxious to collect his ransom as quickly as possible, urged Pizarro to send a detachment there, to collect the treasures that it contained before the priests could hide it.

The journey was long, with two-thirds of it being in the high tablelands of the Cordillera. Fortunately much of the way they were able to travel the main great Inca road that connected Cajamarca with Cuzco, and "nothing in Christendom", exclaimed Hernando Pizarro, "equals the magnificence of this road across the sierra". The road was frequently crossed by streams, which were covered with wooden or slab stone bridges. The wider rivers and chasms were traversed by way of hanging rope bridges, secured on either side by massive stone buttresses. At first the Spaniards were afraid that these bridges would not be able to support the weight of their horses, but they proved to be amazingly resilient.

Modern replica of an Incan rope bridge

Hernando and his men were received all along their journey, with hospitable kindness from the natives. Lodgings were provided, and ample food could be found in the many Tambos that were distributed, at even intervals, along the great road. In many of the towns that they passed through, the inhabitants welcomed them with singing and dancing, and local porters assisted them with carrying their baggage from place to place.

After some weeks, they arrived at Pachacamac, which was a city of a fair size. The temple complex was quite vast in scope and size, with the main buiding resembling more a fortress than a place of worship and pilgrimage. Upon presenting himself at the lower entrance to the temple, Hernando Pizarro was denied entry by the temple guardians. In response, he exclaimed that "he had come too far to be stayed by the arm of an Indian priest", and forced his way into the passage, followed by his men. The passage wound upwards towards the summit, at one end of which stood a small chapel-like structure or room. This was the sanctuary of the deity Pachacamac; the Lord Of The Earthquake.

Entrance to the Sun Temple at Pachacamac

The entrance doorway was decorated with ornaments of crystal , turquoise, and coral. At this moment a tremendous earthquake shook the whole structure violently, causing the natives, both those of the temple and Hernando's men, to flee in terror. However, the Spanish were not deterred by warnings from a mere indian God it seems, for they tore open the door, and entered what they hoped would be a glorious hall filled with gold offered to the deity.

Instead, they found themselves in a small dark apartment or den, filled with the smell of decaying flesh. This was the place of sacrifice to Pachacamac. Once they started to became accommodated with the darkness, they did find a few pieces of gold and some emeralds on the floor, and the effigy of the deity himself; a wooden carving of a good size with a double human face at the top, similar to a Janus. Tearing the sculpture from the room, the Spaniards removed it into the open air and smashed it into a hundred or more fragments. The place was then purified, and a large cross, made of stone and plaster, was erected on the spot.

The native people of the area, seeing that the wrath of Pachacamac was no match for the Spaniards' zeal, or their God, gradually came and submitted to Hernando Pizarro.

He soon found out hereafter that, to his chagrin, the priests of Pachacamac, being forwarned of his arrival and intent, had removed most of the gold and other precious things from the temples, and had hid them. Some of it was soon found nearby, but not all.

One prize, which made up for the lack of golden abundance, was the news that the Indian commander Challcuchima was camped, with a sizeable force, at Xauxu, some distance from Pachacamac. He was a close relative of Atahuallpa, as well as his most experienced general. Along with Quizquiz, who was in Cuzco, Challcuchima had achieved the victories which had put Atahuallpa on the throne of the Tahuantinsuyu.

A messenger from Hernando to Challcuchima stating that he wished to meet with the Inca general was rebuffed, so Hernando decided to take him by force, using the same ploy that the Spanish had used against Atahuallpa.

Xuaxa was a large city by local standards, having a population perhaps as high as 100,000 people. The Incan general was camped a few miles away, with an army of 35,000. With some resistance he agreed

96

to meet with Hernando, who, addressing him courteously, urged him to return with him to Cajamarca, upon orders of his Sapa Inca.

Since the capture of Atahuallpa, Challcuchima was at odds within himself as to what course of action to take in regards to the Sapa Inca's plight. He could not comprehend how such a small group of foreigners had been able to seemingly outwit and overtake his sovereign. Nor did he know what, precisely, Atahuallpa would wish him to do, so, he decided that it was best to meet with his monarch face to face, escorted along the way by Hernando.

Challcuchima arrived at the Spaniards' camp attended by a large retinue. He was borne in a litter on the shoulders of his soldiers, as befit an Incan general, and was received throughout the journey to Cajamarca by the natives with warm greetings and blessings. Upon reaching Cajamarca, he entered the Sapa Inca's quarters in bare feet, and openly wept as he exclaimed, "would that I had been here This would not hare happened".

The emissaries that had been sent to Cuzco to collect gold for Atahuallpa's ransom returned at this time. Owing to the Inca's orders that the Spanish be given safe passage, they were treated in an almost imperial manner by the inhabitants.

They travelled all the way from Cajamarca to Cuzco along the main Inca road, not on foot or horseback, but in the litters or Hamacas usually reserved for Inca royalty. Over the course of the 600 miles of this journey, they were relayed by teams of carriers fro beginning to end. Upon reaching Cuzco, the inhabitants celebrated the arrival of the Spaniards with public festivities, and their every want was taken care of.

Their accounts to Pizarro of the sophistication and wealth of the city, especially the latter, confirmed the stories that he had heard earlier. The great temple of the sun, Coricancha, had an interior literally covered with plates of gold. They immediately demanded these be removed, and the temples attendants did so reluctantly, but knew that by doing so, would help in the release of their sovereign.

The number of plates removed was approximately 700, each one being a square foot in size. Where was the rest, they insisted? Surely there must be more temples in the city than just this one. Unfortunately, Pizarro had sent three of his most uncouth soldiers to carry out this enterprise. They treated the local populace with disdain, and reputably even entered the convent of the Virgins of the Sun and had their way with them. The people of Cuzco were so offended by the crude actions of these men, and wished to violently attack them, but had been told that they had been sent there by order of Atahuallpa himself, and thus their demands had to be honoured.

Royal Incan ornamente and 2 quero, that fortumately escaped being melted down by the spanish

Once these emissaries had collected as much gold as could be transported back to Cajamarca, they left, much to the relief of the citizens of Cuzco. And although it was not enough to secure Atahuallpa's release, it was still sizeable. Unfortunately, the 700 gold sheets, when stacked one on top of the other, did not make up that great a volume.

Just prior to the above, Almagro returned from Panama with fresh re-enforcements, numbering 150 soldiers, and 50 horses. It was now february 1533. Pizarro was overjoyed with the arrival of these new troops, for now, he felt, he could go forward with the conquest of the entire Tahuantinsuyu.

There was one person in Cajamarca who was not as pleased about Almagro's arrival as were the others, and that was Atahuallpa. With this sudden increase in the foreigner's numbers, he began to worry more about his future, and that of the Tahuantinsuyu. A remarkable occurrence in the sky, pointed out to him by Pizarro's soldiers, was the presence of a meteor, or perhaps a comet. He gazed at it for several minutes, and then said, with a sense of foreboding, that "a similar sign had been seen in the skies a short time before the death of his father Huyana Capac".

Pizarro was eager to push forward towards Cuzco, but one obstacle stood in his way; the ransom of Atahuallpa. Although a huge quantity of gold had been collected, it was not yet the full amount. The Spanish soldiers, upon seeing the vast treasure brought back from Cuzco, insisted that it be divided amongst them, now. Also, they collectively wished to march to Cuzco as soon as possible, to prevent the citizens of that city from hiding what gold remained. Pizarro agreed, and knew that without having the capital under his complete control, he could not hope to capture and secure the whole Tahuantinsuyu.

Thus, he set about dividing the spoils, which was problematic from the very start, because the gold was not uniform in any way. It consisted of a variety of objects, from goblets, vases, ornaments, tiles, plates, and utensils of different sizes, shapes, and degrees of purity.

The only way to establish a uniform grade of distribution was to melt it all down into ingots of one shape and weight. So, the beautiful artistic expressions of many of the Tahuantinsuyu's greatest jewelers and metal sculptors, including exacting replicas of ears of corn, which were sheathed in broad leaves of silver, and even the silk was lovingly re-created, were melted down into anonymous bricks. Fortunately, for the artists' legacy, at least, the one-fifth to be paid to Charles, the King Of Spain, as his share and tribute, was left intact.

The melting down of the art treasures was entrusted to the native goldsmiths, to undo what they had previously created. This task was carried out day and night, and took an entire month before all of the gold was thus transformed. It was immediately distributed amongst all of Pizarro's men, portions being decided by the commander himself, based upon rank and effectiveness of service.

All thoughts then turned towards Cuzco, but, what to do with Atahuallpa? To set him free could result in his re-ascendancy to the throne, and thereby rally the entire Tahuantinsuyu behind him. To keep him prisoner in Cajamarca would mean keeping many troops behind as guards, thus reducing the ranks required for their forward actions. And to take him with them? Well, that would make them an obvious target of attack.

Atahuallpa himself now loudly demanded his freedom. Even though the full ransom had not been met, the majority of the Spanish wanted to push on to Cuzco. But rumours rose again of a possible native uprising. This time, it was said that Atahuallpa's forces were stirring to the north, in Quito, planning to attack the Spanish, and secure the Sapa Inca's release. The source of the rumours was unknown, but may have actually been made up of natives in Atahuallpa's own group, who held secreted support for Huascar.

In any event, all Spanish fingers pointed to Atahuallpa as the author of the uprising. Challcuchima was interrogated on the subject, which he denounced and called malicious slander. Pizarro then grilled the Sapa Inca himself, already believing the rumours to be truth. "What treason is this", he said, "that you have meditated against me, me, who have treated you with honour, confiding in your words, as those of a brother?" "You jest", replied Atahuallpa, "you are always jesting with me. How could I or my people think of conspiring against men so valiant as the Spaniards? Do not jest with me thus, I beseech you". "This", continues Pizarro's secretary, who wrote down the whole conversation, "he said in the most composed and natural manner, smiling all the while to dissemble his falsehood, so that we were all amazed to find such cunning in a barbarian".

But it was not with cunning, but the consciousness of innocence, that caused Atahuallpa to speak. "Am I not", he said to Pizarro, "a poor captive in your hands? How could I harbour the designs you impute to me, when I should be the first victim of the outbreak? And you little know my people, if you think that such a movement would be made without my orders; when the very birds in my dominions, would scarcely venture to fly contrary to my will".

The rumours of a possible native insurrection grew. A large force, it was said, had already gathered at Huamachuco, less than one hundred miles from Cajamarca, and an attack was immanent. Many of the Spaniards called for the immediate execution of Atahuallpa. Amongst these was Almagro, who had not been on the scene for the Sapa Inca's capture, but regarded him as an encumbrance to the forward movement of the Spanish enterprise, and of his own fortunes, because little gold had been found in Cajamarca.

Pizarro refused this drastic demand, and was in this supported by Hernando de Soto. In order to ascertain whether the rumours were true or not, the Spanish commander sent a small contingent, headed by de Soto, to Huamachuco. The matter should thereby be resolved within a few days.

Upon de Soto's departure, instead of the animosity towards Atahuallpa subsiding, it grew worse. Pizarro felt that he had no choice but to bring the Sapa Inca to trial immediately. A court was convened, with Pizarro and Almagro presiding as judges. The charges laid against Atahuallpa were 12 in number, the most important being: that he had stolen the crown and assassinated his brother Huascar; squandered the public revenues since the conquest of the country by the Spaniards; was guilty of idolatry, adultery, and polygamy; and finally, had attempted to incite an insurrection against the Spaniards.

A number of indian witnesses were brought forward and questioned, through the interpreter Felipillo, who greatly despised Atahuallpa, and the results were clearly less than truthful.

The Sapa Inca was found guilty, and was sentenced to be burned alive in the plaza of Cajamarca that very night. It was desirable to receive the blessings of the priest Father Valverde to this judgement, and upon receiving a copy, he immediately signed it without hesitation, declaring that, "in his opinion, the Inca, at all events, deserved death".

When the sentence was read out to Atahuallpa, he was greatly overcome. With tears in his eyes he exclaimed, "What have I done, or my children, that I should meet such a fate? And from your hands, to", addressing Pizarro, "you, who have met with friendship and kindness from my people, with whom I have shared my treasures, who have received nothing but benefits from my hands".

Two hours before sunset, on august 29, 1533, Atahuallpa was led out into the plaza, chained hand and foot. Father Valverde was at his side, administering consolation, and hoping to persuade the Sapa Inca, in his final hour, to renounce the religion of his ancestors, and embrace Christianity. Throughout his imprisonment, the friar had expounded the teachings and virtues of the Christian faith to Atahuall-pa, and although the latter did learn many good things, he could not expunge his ancestors belief system from his heart.

The Dominican priest made one final appeal, as the flickering fires began to surround the tied up Inca, stating that, if Atahuallpa were to be baptised now, he would be spared from his present state, and instead be strangled by garrotting. His last wishes were that his re-mains be returned to Quito, to lay with his maternal ancestors, and that Pizarro take compassion on his children and take them under his protectful care.

Spanish pen and ink sketch of the execution of Atahuallpa

A day or two after these events, Hernando de Soto returned from Huamachuco. He was greatly astonished and outraged upon hearing of Atahuallpa's execution. Upon seeking out and finding Pizarro, who was clearly in a state of mourning, de Soto declared, "you have acted rashly. Atahuallpa has been slandered. There was no enemy at

Huamachaco; no rising among the natives. I have met nothing on the road but demonstrations of good-will, and all is quiet. If it was necessary to bring the Inca to trial, he should have been taken to Castille and judged by the emperor. I would have pledged myself to see him safe on board the vessel".

As has already been stated, the Sapa Inca was not a ceremonial title; he was not simply the head of the state, but the point and pinnacle to which all of the institutions converged. With him as the capstone, the whole structure must collapse, as it did after Atahuallpa's death. With no immediate successor appointed to his position, and with the whole of the Tahuantinsuyu's population being told that a stronger foreign hand now held the sceptre of power, it was clear that the dynasty of the Inca, birthed from the waters of Lake Titicaca, was now dead.

The consequences of this were immediate and devastating. The beautifully orchestrated institutions, and social order, so carefully nurtured and coordinated, simply fell apart. Villages were burned, temples and palaces were plundered, and the gold that they contained was scattered and secreted, not by the Spanish, but by the natives themselves. The precious metals, which prior to the Spaniards' arrival held only ceremonial importance, now had a monetary value in the eyes of the indians.

The outer provinces now shook off their allegiance to the Inca, and the heads of some of the remote armies, set up for themselves. The whole of the Tahuantinsuyu began to crumble. Pizarro felt that the only way to instil some sort of social order was to appoint a successor. The obvious choice was Huascar's younger brother, Manco, but he was thought to be residing in Cuzco. Thus, Toparca, who was Atahuallpa's younger brother, and was residing in Cajamarca, was appointed, with as much ceremony and pomp as would allow. As most of the natives present were from Quito and thus previously devoted to Atahuallpa, Toparca was a popular choice, locally at least.

All thoughts now turned to Cuzco. With a company of nearly 500 men, one third cavalry, Pizarro set off fom Cajamarca in september. They travelled the great Inca road, and all along this route, at regular intervals, took advantage of the Tambos which were filled with grain and other useful commodities.

Numerous skirmishes with localized forces occurred during the journey, but none that truly fazed the Spaniards. Full blame for these acts of opposition were pointed at the hand of the general Challcuchima, who was a captive member of the travelling party. He was immediately executed.

The most unfortunate event was the sudden and inexplicable death of Toparca. As fate, perhaps, would have it, Pizarro was surprised soon after by a visit from the young prince Manco, Huascar's brother. Manco announced his claim to the throne, and asked for the Spaniards' protection, for although he claimed to be the instigator of the recent military clashes, since they had been ineffective, he had chosen this new political course.

Pizarro listened with interest to the young prince's words, and whether they were true or not, saw in Manco the most useful Incan tool that he could employ in quelling the natives' hostilities, and furthering his own personal ambitions. Accordingly, he not only received this new Sapa Inca candidate with great warmth, but assured him that he, Pizarro, had been sent to this country by his Castilian emperor to vindicate the claims of Huascar to the crown, and to punish all those opposed to this task.

The Spanish commander, and his newly expanded entourage, caught their first glimpse of Cuzco late that afternoon. The golden beams of the waning God Inti shone on the polished surfaces of the multitude of low-lying buildings of the capital city, and as darness encroached, Pizarro chose to wait until the next morning to enter this greatest of treasures.

On november 15, 1533, Pizarro and his army entered Cuzco, and set up camp in the main square; the present-day Plaza de Armas. Though falling short of the El Dorado with which the Spanish had affixed their wildest fantasies, they were truly impressed by the beauty of the buildings, the length and regularity of its streets, and the grace and sophistication of its inhabitants.

The population at that time was estimated at 200,000 with more in the suburbs (the present population is approximately 450,000).

"In the delicacy of the stone-work", stated one of the Spaniards, "the natives far excelled the Spaniards, though the roofs of their dwellings, instead of tiles, were only of thatch, but put together with the nicest art". This was partly due to the fact that Cuzco received very little rain, so tile or stone roofing was innecessary.

The author dwarfed by stone wall of Sachsayhuaman

The most impressive, and largest of all of the buildings was the great fortress and religious center of Sacsayhuaman, which even to this day looms on a hill above the city. But the most beautiful and most ornate was the Coricancha, or Sun Temple, which was surrounded by other buildings of a religious nature, such as that for the Virgins of the Sun.

Upon entering Cuzco, Pizarro had issued strict orders forbidding any of his officers from damaging or looting from any of the dwellings. But his troops lost no time in plundering the palaces, and defacing the religious works found inside. They stripped the gems and gold from the royal mummies in the Coricancha, and tortured local people who refused to give information about the places where valuable artefacts had been secreted away.

The whole mass of treasure, or at least most of it, was put into a common heap, like in Cajamarca, and after the one-fifth for the crown had been removed, was melted down as before. In all, the spoils greatly exceeded that of Atahuallpa's ransom.

The treasure was divided between the 480 of Pizarro's men, the amounts depending upon their rank and extent of service. Some of these soldiers, never having seen or been in possession of such wealth in a transferable form in their lives, took to gambling with one another. In one special case, that of a cavalry officer named Leguizano, whose payment was the sacred gold image of the Sun God Inti torn from the wall of the Coricancha, lost it, through gambling, in a single night. From this came a famous Spanish proverb: Juega el Sol antes que amanezca, "He plays away the Sun before sunrise".

After the division of the treasures of Cuzco, Pizarro got to work to re-establish civil obedience and thus control. In front of a large crowd, he presented Manco, son of Huayna Capac, and legitimate heir to the throne of the Tahuantinsuyu and its people. The citizens of Cuzco rejoiced, believing that their sacred Inca monarchy had been restored.

The ceremony of ascension was carried out in explicit detail, with a few new Spanish twists. The Incan nobles, general populace, and the entire Spanish army all assembled in the great square as witnesses. Father Valverde, and not an Incan priest, performed the religious aspects of the ritual, while Pizarro placed the royal fringed diadem on Manco's forehead. As the climax to the event, the Spanish royal notary read aloud a document asserting the supremacy of the Castilian crown.

Pizarro's next move was to place his people in the top places of power in the city. On the 24th of march, 1534, in front of Spanish and Natives alike, two mayors for the city of Cuzco were presented (his people of course). Father Valverde, now the Bishop of Cuzco, was given the Coricancha in which to establish a monastery, and a large spot on the edge of the main plaza for his cathedral. The House of the Virgins of the Sun, was replaced by a Roman Catholic Nunnery.

On the military front, Pizarro, now Governor Pizarro, received repeated accounts of a sizeable native force forming on the outskirts of the capital, under the command of Atahuallpa's general Quizquiz. Almagro, with a small body of horses and a large native force under the Inca Manco, clashed with Quizquiz and his troops, beating them back to Xauxa. The superior force of the Spanish, combined with Manco's warriors who had previously fought under Huascar, continued to push Quizquiz and his mainly Atahuallpan dedicated troops all the way to Quito.

Weary from the onslaught of the enemy, Quizquiz's own men then massacred him in cold blood.

With Cuzco now ruled by Spanish politicians, the Catholics in control of all religious undertakings, the military broken into factions, and a puppet Inca on the throne, there could be no revival of renaissance of the great Tahuantinsuyu; Inti descended behind the hills as darkness fell, and rose the next morning not as a God in the minds and hearts of most, but simply a celestial orb.

The rule of the Spanish, began early in the 16th century, is still clearly present today, early in the 21st. The highest positions in government, religion, finance and military continue to be mainly occupied by people of Spanish descent.

The Inti Raymi, a celebration of the winter solstice, is still celebrated to this day

The great majority of the native population of Peru live in poverty, whether in Lima, other cities, or on the lands of their ancestors.

Direct descendants of the Inca still exist, in dwindling numbers. They still only marry amongst themselves, in order to preserve the divine bloodline. One graceful old lady, now in her 90's, is the last human being on earth to bear the surname Pachacutec.

Yet other echoes and whispers of the Inca still remain. Travellers on the Pan American highway, from Santiago de Chile, in the south, to Tumbes in the north of Peru, are actually traversing the ancient Incan

Road. The main temples and palaces of Cuzco, or at least their sturdy foundations, are still in remarkable states of preservation.

More than 2,000,000 native Peruvians still speak Runa Simi, the language of the Inca. And, as I finish this book, in February of 2010, more than 10,000 homes around Cuzco have recently been destroyed as a result of devastating rains and flooding by the sacred Vilcanota river. Yet the citadel of Machu Picchu, along with other major temples such as Ollantaytambo, stand perfectly intact, thanks to the ingenious drainage systems designed and built more than 500 years ago.

As earthquakes over time have damaged or even destroyed Spanish structures built on top of the foundations of Incan temples, the Incan walls remain strong and intact. Let us hope that the founding principles and examples set forth by the Inca live for at least another 500 years in the hearts and minds of Peruvians and visitors alike.

UNA BREVE HISTORIA DE LOS INCAS

Se terminó de imprimir en los
Talleres Gráficos de CMYK IMPRESORES SAC.
TELEFAX: 461 4575
E-mail: cmykimpresores@yahoo.com

Lima, Perú

Made in the USA
San Bernardino, CA
14 November 2013